KU-364-393

The Emerging British Underclass

Charles Murray

Frank Field
Joan C. Brown
Nicholas Deakin
Alan Walker

CHESTER COLLEGE

ACC. No.
915309 01

DEPT.

CLASS No.
305.5690942 MUR

LIBRARY

London
The IEA Health and Welfare Unit
1990

First published in May 1990
by
The IEA Health and Welfare Unit
2 Lord North St
London SW1P 3LB

© The IEA Health and Welfare Unit 1990

All rights reserved

ISBN 0-255 36263-3

Typeset by the IEA Health and Welfare Unit
Printed in Great Britain by
Goron Pro-Print Co. Ltd
Churchill Industrial Estate, Lancing, West Sussex

Accession no LG
915309 01
TELEPEN

The IEA Health and Welfare Unit

Choice in Welfare Series No. 2

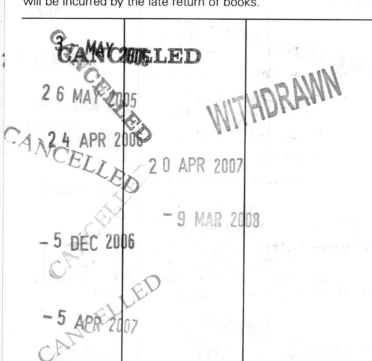

CHESTER CAMPUS
LIBRARY
01244 392738

This book is to be returned on or before the
last date stamped below. Overdue charges
will be incurred by the late return of books.

UNIVERSITY COLLEGE
CHESTER

CANCELLED

2 6 MAY 2005

2 4 APR 2006

2 0 APR 2007

- 9 MAR 2008

- 5 DEC 2006

- 5 APR 2007

WITHDRAWN

The publication of this book
has been made possible by a grant from

John Spiers

Contents

Foreword

Charles Murray's *Underclass* was first published in the *Sunday Times Magazine* in November 1989 and we are now making it available in a more permanent form. The IEA's goal is to provide materials which can be used for teaching in schools, colleges, polytechnics and universities whilst also remaining accessible to the general reader and, to increase the value of Murray's paper as a teaching aid, it is being published with four commentaries by leading critics of his point of view. Charles Murray replies to their criticisms and develops his argument in a Rejoinder.

Murray takes pains to explain that he does not apply the term underclass to all the poor, only to those distinguished by their undesirable behaviour, including drug-taking, crime, illegitimacy, failure to hold down a job, truancy from school and casual violence. He concentrates on three measures: crime, dropping out of the labour force and illegitimacy. He believes that illegitimacy is the best indicator of an underclass in the making and the rising trend of illegitimacy therefore alarms him. He contends that it is better that children should have two parents rather than one but believes there is a radical difference between different single-parent situations. Unlike divorce or widowhood, illegitimacy is a special problem, he says, because there is a single parent from day one and the child has not been the first consideration of the parents and may indeed be regarded as a mere encumbrance.

Crime too is growing and Murray cites with some amazement the statistic that there is more property crime in England and Wales than the US. His special concern, however, is crimes of violence particulary where whole neighbourhoods fall prey to criminality to such an extent that it becomes impossible for parents to raise their children to be unaggressive. No less alarming, Murray finds that a proportion of those who left school in the 1980s were not socialised into the world of work. He does not worry about this merely because other workers have to keep them at the public expense, but for their own sakes. Work is at the centre of life and without it, individuals are hard pressed to acquire and maintain both self-esteem and the respect of others. There is more to work than just making a living, says Murray.

Murray's assessment is that Britain has an underclass and that it is growing. He is frequently criticised for not offering a ready-made set of policies for governments to implement. The reason he refuses to prescribe alternative policies in detail is that, after spending much of his life implementing and appraising reform programmes, he has become pessimistic about the capacity of governments to engineer solutions at all. Providing jobs and training is not enough, he thinks, nor is tinkering with the benefit system sufficient. According to Murray, the only remedy is authentic self-government by local communities.

Murray's paper is published with four commentaries. Labour MP, Frank Field does not resist the use of the term underclass but defines it differently from Murray. In his view, it comprises three groups: the frail-elderly pensioner, single parents, and the long-term unemployed. Field's primary concern is to reduce inequalities of income and wealth, whilst the essence of Murray's approach is that a distinction should be made between low income as such and the behavioural poverty that results from conduct which is both anti-social and self-harming.

Joan Brown's paper challenges Murray's claim that single unmarried mothers constitute a special problem, pointing out that, according to a study by Ermisch, divorced mothers as a group spend longer on benefit than unwed mothers and that never-married mothers remain lone parents for a shorter average period than divorced mothers. Murray explains in his Rejoinder why he finds the Ermisch study wanting.

Alan Walker's essay is a forthright and unyielding statement of his socialist standpoint. He is an unrepentant egalitarian whose final assessment is that Murray's underclass theory 'blames the victim' and thus diverts our attention from blaming the mechanisms through which resources are distributed. Victim blaming is an attitude which Walker believes to have been at the root of many measures from the Elizabethan poor law to today's YTS and Restart programmes.

Professor Deakin's essay is dismissive and disdainful in tone, a tradition of social-policy writing popularised by Titmuss. His scorn for Murray leads him to conclude that he is advocating a kind of authoritarianism — 'a static form of society composed of neatly docketed and differentiated small units from which the dangerous classes have been carefully excluded'. Some readers may find this claim a little audacious, since it is flatly contradicted by everything that Murray has ever said or written.

In his Rejoinder. Murray offers a vigorous and good-humoured defence. He urges the necessity to conduct detailed sociological, one might say anthropological, studies in the field to bring investigators into face-to-face contact with the facts of human conduct; and he points to the dangers of relying too heavily on statistical interpretations which blur distinctions and conceal complexity by aggregation.

Individual Freedom and Criticising the Poor

Finally, may I add a word of explanation for those who ask why classical liberals should be interested in these issues at all. What has individual freedom got to do with criticising the poor? The most important reason is that you cannot have a free society without morally-responsible citizens and you cannot have morally-responsible citizens unless we all take the trouble to tell each other when we are at fault and when we are doing well. People are fallible and we need the constant attention and support of others to keep us on the straight-and-narrow. That is why classical liberals mistrust political power. In Acton's oft-quoted words, 'Power tends to corrupt, and absolute power corrupts absolutely'. The classical-liberal remedy is government based on checks and balances and openness to criticism. Similarly, in economics human beings are fallible and may err on the side of selfishness. Classical liberals urge competition to check this tendency and direct possibly selfish energies into the service of others. Human beings are no less fallible in private life, and here it is the praise or blame of others mediated by conscience, or what Adam Smith called the impartial spectator, which guides us.

Yet in social policy it is considered inhumane to criticise or blame an individual who has fallen into hardship due to his own conduct. The humane approach is assumed to be the giving of money to the poor; anything else amounts to making excuses for not giving them money and is, accordingly, inhumane. But can it legitimately be claimed that to pass judgement on a person's conduct is automatically uncaring?

Consider the opposite of blame, praise. When we praise someone we applaud their achievement. We do so primarily to encourage still greater effort and achievement. Is blame not similar? We blame, we criticise, we judge, we censure in order to encourage people to do better next time. For years the *bête noire* of the social-policy mainstream has been stigma, which originally meant a mark branded on a slave or criminal. Social policies have been designed and redesigned in the hope of avoiding stigma. And to avoid stigmatising someone appears at first sight to be humane because it would be wholly wrong to brand someone a failure, or to stain their character permanently.

But if we criticise a person who has fallen on hard times due to their own inappropriate behaviour, we do not brand them failures in some absolute or permanent sense. We spend our time criticising them because we believe them capable of more. Failure never hurt anyone because it is through our failures as well as our successes that we grow. To criticise a person is to treat him as a dignified individual capable of functioning as a morally-responsible citizen. To refrain from criticising individuals whose conduct may be self-injuring as well as harmful to others, is in a fundamental sense to write them off as not worth bothering with. It is to treat them as the powerless victims of circumstance and thus to fail to acknowledge the very capacity that makes us all human, our ability to act as thinking, valuing, choosing individuals.

We can learn something from our forbears about combining humanity with praise and blame. It might well be callous to refuse to help someone on the ground that they were the author of their own misfortune. People should be helped whether or not they are to blame, wholly or partly for their own predicament. The important question is *how* they should be helped. In the days when self-help was the norm and the majority joined mutual aid societies to make provision against hard times, callous disregard for the unfortunate was denounced. The Manchester Unity friendly society, a million-strong voluntary association of workers for mutual aid and one of many similar organisations the membership of which far outnumbered that of the trade unions until the Second World War, enjoined its members to combine caring with criticism:

> In extending our charity we must endeavour to distinguish the really deserving, for those who willingly and professionally seek the charity of others forfeit all self-respect, and, in being content so to live, sacrifice personal dignity.

The duty of the Manchester Unity member in such cases was to try to awaken the 'love of independence'. But, this was not a policy of callous disregard:

> those who unworthily seek assistance are not to be neglected if really in distress; the voice of misery, proceed from whence it may, should never be disregarded. However, after relieving the actual wants of these unhappy persons, we should endeavour to raise them from the degradation into which they have fallen, and make them richer in their own esteem. As it is better that ten guilty persons escape than that one innocent should suffer, so it is better that ten undeserving persons be assisted than that one worthy be neglected.

To refrain from judging people is to refrain from respecting them. Perhaps it is time for social policy analysts to adopt a new rallying cry: Bring back stigma; all is forgiven!

David G. Green

Acknowledgement

We are very grateful to *The Sunday Times* for making possible Charles Murray's period of study in Britain in 1989, and to Andrew Neil, Editor of *The Sunday Times*, for granting permission to reproduce Charles Murray's article which originally appeared in *The Sunday Times Magazine* on 26 November 1989.

The Authors

Charles Murray is a social scientist and writer. He is the author of *Losing Ground: American Social Policy 1950-1980* (1984) and *In Pursuit: Of Happiness and Good Government* (1988).

Murray is Bradley Fellow with the Manhattan Institute for Policy Research. In addition to his books, Murray has written widely in *The Public Interest, Commentary, The Atlantic, The New Republic, The Wilson Quarterly, Political Science Quarterly, National Review, American Spectator, The Wall Street Journal,* and *The New York Times*. In 1989, he and his wife, Catherine Cox, published *Apollo: The Race to the Moon*, an account of the programme that achieved the first lunar landing. He is currently at work on a new book in collaboration with Professor Richard Herrnstein of Harvard University.

From 1974 through 1981, Murray was a senior scientist at the American Institutes for Research (AIR), one of the largest of the private social science research organizations. At AIR, Murray supervised evaluations in the fields of urban education, welfare services, day care, adolescent pregnancy, services for the elderly, and criminal justice. Before joining AIR, Murray spent six years in Thailand, first as a Peace Corps Volunteer attached to the Village Health program, then as a researcher in rural Thailand.

Murray was born and raised in Newton, Iowa. He obtained a B.A. in history from Harvard and a Ph.D. in political science from the Massachusetts Institute of Technology. He lives with his wife and children near Washington, DC.

Frank Field has been the Labour Member of Parliament for Birkenhead since 1979. He is currently Chairman of the Select Committee on Social Services and is Opposition Spokesman on the Church.

His publications include: *The Minimum Wage: its Potential and Dangers* (1984); *Freedom and Wealth in a Socialist Future* (1987);

The Politics of Paradise (1987); *Losing Out: The Emergence of Britain's Underclass* (1989).

Joan C. Brown is an independent researcher in social policy and was formerly employed as a Senior Research Fellow at the Policy Studies Institute. Her principal interests are social security and poverty, both in the UK and in the European Community. Earlier in her career she worked in Australia and Canada and she retains an interest in developments in these countries.

While at the Policy Studies Institute, Joan Brown had a series of studies published on issues for family income support, disability income and occupational benefits. Since 1988, her published studies have included: *In Search of a Policy: the Rationale for Social Security Provision for One-Parent Families* (1988); *Child Benefit: Investing in the Future* (1988); a study for the Social Security Advisory Committee entitled *Why Don't They Go to Work? Mothers on Benefit* (1989); and most recently *Victims or Villains? Social Security Benefits in Unemployment*, (1990).

Alan Walker is Professor of Social Policy and Chairperson of the Department of Sociological Studies, University of Sheffield. He is also a Director of the University's Policy Studies Centre. He has taught at the University of Sheffield since 1977 and has held the Chair of Social Policy since 1985.

Professor Walker is sole author, co-author, or editor of ten books, including *Unqualified and Underemployed* (1982); *Social Planning* (1984); *Ageing and Social Policy* (ed. with C. Phillipson; 1986) and *After Redundancy* (with I. Noble and J. Westergaard; 1989). He has also contributed numerous articles and chapters to learned journals and edited books in social policy and social gerontology. He is currently engaged in two major field research studies — one is on the employment of older workers and the other is an evaluation of a new form of social care for elderly people being pioneered in Sheffield.

Nicholas Deakin has been Professor of Social Policy and Administration at Birmingham University since 1980. Previously, he worked first as a civil servant and then on a research programme in race relations funded by the Nuffield Foundation. After spending three years in the late 1960s researching and teaching at Sussex University, he went back to work in government, where he served as Head of the Central Policy Unit at the GLC.

Professor Deakin has published numerous books and articles on race relations, urban policy and new towns. His most recent publications are *The Politics of Welfare*, (1987) and *Community Public Services* (with A.W. Wright and others, 1990).

1

UNDERCLASS

Charles Murray

The Concept of 'Underclass'

'Underclass' is an ugly word, with its whiff of Marx and the lumpenproletariat. Perhaps because it is ugly, 'underclass' as used in Britain tends to be sanitised, a sort of synonym for people who are not just poor, but especially poor. So let us get it straight from the outset: the 'underclass' does not refer to degree of poverty, but to a type of poverty.

It is not a new concept. I grew up knowing what the underclass was; we just didn't call it that in those days. In the small Iowa town where I lived, I was taught by my middle-class parents that there were two kinds of poor people. One class of poor people was never even called 'poor'. I came to understand that they simply lived with low incomes, as my own parents had done when they were young. Then there was another set of poor people, just a handful of them. These poor people didn't lack just money. They were defined by their behaviour. Their homes were littered and unkempt. The men in the family were unable to hold a job for more than a few weeks at a time. Drunkenness was common. The children grew up ill-schooled and ill-behaved and contributed a disproportionate share of the local juvenile delinquents.

British observers of the 19th century knew these people. To Henry Mayhew, whose articles in the *Morning Chronicle* in 1850 drew the Victorians' attention to poverty, they were the 'dishonest poor', a member of which was distinguished from the civilised man by his repugnance to regular and continuous labour — by his want of providence in laying up a store for the future — by his inability to perceive consequences ever so slightly removed from immediate apprehensions — by his passion for stupefying herbs and roots and, when possible, for intoxicating fermented liquors...

Other popular labels were 'undeserving', 'unrespectable', 'depraved', 'debased', 'disreputable' or 'feckless' poor.

As Britain entered the 1960s a century later, this distinction between honest and dishonest poor people had been softened. The second kind of poor person was no longer 'undeserving'; rather, he was the product of a 'culture of poverty'. But intellectuals as well as the man in the street continued to accept that poor people were not all alike. Most were doing their best under difficult circumstances; a small number were pretty much as Mayhew had described them. Then came the intellectual reformation that swept both the United States and Britain at about the same time, in the mid-1960s, and with it came a new way of looking at the poor. Henceforth, the poor were to be homogenised. The only difference between poor people and everyone else, we were told, was that the poor had less money. More importantly, the poor were all alike. There was not such thing as the ne'er-do-well poor person — he was the figment of the prejudices of a parochial middle class. Poor people, *all* poor people, were equally victims, and would be equally successful if only society gave them a fair shake.

The Difference between the US and the UK

The difference between the United States and Britain was that the United States reached the future first. During the last half of the 1960s and throughout the 1970s something strange and frightening was happening among poor people in the United States. Poor communities that had consisted mostly of hardworking folks began deteriorating, sometimes falling apart altogether. Drugs, crime, illegitimacy, homelessness, drop-out from the job market, drop-out from school, casual violence — all the measures that were available to the social scientists showed large increases, focused in poor communities. As the 1980s began, the growing population of 'the other kind of poor people' could no longer be ignored, and a label for them came into use. In the US, we began to call them the underclass.

For a time, the intellectual conventional wisdom continued to hold that 'underclass' was just another pejorative attempt to label the poor. But the label had come into use because there was no longer any denying reality. What had once been a small fraction of the American poor had become a sizeable and worrisome population. An underclass existed, and none of the ordinary kinds of social policy solutions seemed able to stop its growth. One by one, the American social scientists who had initially rejected the concept of an underclass fell silent, then began to use it themselves.

By and large, British intellectuals still disdain the term. In 1987, the social historian John Macnicol summed up the prevailing view in the *Journal of Social Policy*,[1] writing dismissively that underclass was nothing more than a refuted concept periodically resurrected by Conservatives 'who wish to constrain the redistributive potential of state welfare'. But there are beginning to be breaks in the ranks. Frank Field, the prominent Labour MP, has just published a book with 'underclass' in its subtitle. The newspapers, watching the United States and seeing shadows of its problems in Britain, have begun to use the term. As someone who has been analysing this phenomenon in the United States, I arrived in Britain earlier this year, a visitor from a plague area come to see whether the disease is spreading.

With all the reservations that a stranger must feel in passing judgement on an unfamiliar country, I will jump directly to the conclusion: Britain does have an underclass, still largely out of sight and still smaller than the one in the United States. But it is growing rapidly. Within the next decade, it will probably

[1] Vol. 16, No. 3, pp. 293-318.

4

become as large (proportionately) as the United States' underclass. It could easily become larger.

I am not talking here about an unemployment problem that can be solved by more jobs, nor about a poverty problem that can be solved by higher benefits. Britain has a growing population of working-aged, healthy people who live in a different world from other Britons, who are raising their children to live in it, and whose values are now contaminating the life of entire neighbourhoods — which is one of the most insidious aspects of the phenomenon, for neighbours who don't share those values cannot isolate themselves.

There are many ways to identify an underclass. I will concentrate on three phenomena that have turned out to be early-warning signals in the United States: illegitimacy, violent crime, and drop-out from the labour force. In each case I will be using the simplest of data, collected and published by Britain's Government Statistical Service. I begin with illegitimacy, which in my view is the best predictor of an underclass in the making.

Illegitimacy and the Underclass

It is a proposition that angers many people. Why should it be a 'problem' that a woman has a child without a husband? Why isn't a single woman perfectly capable of raising a healthy, happy child, if only the state will provide a decent level of support so that she may do so? Why is raising a child without having married any more of a problem than raising a child after a divorce? The very world 'illegitimate' is intellectually illegitimate. Using it in a gathering of academics these days is a *faux pas*, causing pained silence.

I nonetheless focus on illegitimacy rather than on the more general phenomenon of one-parent families because, in a world where all social trends are ambiguous, illegitimacy is less ambiguous than other forms of single parenthood. It is a matter of degree. Of course some unmarried mothers are excellent mothers and some unmarried fathers are excellent fathers. Of course some divorced parents disappear from the children's lives altogether and some divorces have more destructive effects on the children than a failure to marry would have had. Being without two parents is generally worse for the child than having two parents, no matter how it happens. But illegitimacy is the purest form of being without two parents — legally, the child is without a father from day one; he is often without one practically as well. Further, illegitimacy bespeaks an attitude on the part of one or both parents that getting married is not an essential part of siring or giving birth to a child; this in itself distinguishes their mindset from that of people who do feel strongly that getting married is essential.

Call it what you will, illegitimacy has been sky-rocketing since 1979. I use 'sky-rocketing' advisedly. In Figure 1 for the years since the Second World War ended, the post-war era divides into three parts. From the end of the Second World War until 1960, Britain enjoyed a very low and even slightly declining illegitimacy ratio. From 1960 until 1978 the ratio increased, but remained modest by international standards — as late as 1979, Britain's illegitimacy ratio was only 10.6 per cent, one of the lowest rates in the industrialised West. Then, suddenly, during a period when fertility was steady, the illegitimacy ratio began to rise very rapidly — to 14.1 per cent by 1982, 18.9 per cent by 1985, and finally to 25.6 per cent by 1988. If present trends continue, Britain will pass the United States in this unhappy statistic in 1990.

The sharp rise is only half of the story. The other and equally important half is that illegitimate births are not scattered evenly among the British population. In this, press reports can be misleading. There is much publicity about the member of the royal family who has a child without a husband, or the socially prominent young career woman who deliberately decides to have a baby on her own, but these are comparatively rare events. The increase in illegitimate births is strikingly concentrated among the lowest social class.

Municipal Districts

This is especially easy to document in Britain, where one may fit together the Government Statistical Service's birth data on municipal districts with the detailed socio-economic data from the general census. When one does so for 169 metropolitan districts and boroughs in England and Wales with data from both sources, the relationship between social class and illegitimacy is so obvious that the statistical tests become superfluous. Municipal districts with high concentrations of household heads in Class I (professional persons, by the classification used for many years by the Government Statistical Service) have illegitimacy ratios in the low teens (Wokingham was lowest as of 1987, with only nine of every 100 children born illegitimate) while municipalities like Nottingham and Southwark, with populations most heavily weighed with Class V household heads (unskilled labourers), have illegitimacy ratios of more than 40 per cent (the highest in 1987 was Lambeth, with 46 per cent).

The statistical tests confirm this relationship. The larger the proportion of people who work at unskilled jobs and the larger the proportion who are out of the labour force, the higher the illegitimacy ratio, in a quite specific and regular numeric relationship. The strength of the relationship may be illustrated this way: suppose you were limited to two items of information about a community — the percentage of people in Class V and the percentage of people who are 'economically inactive'. With just these two measures, you could predict the illegitimacy ratio, usually within just three percentage points of the true number. As a statistician might summarise it, these two measures of economic status 'explain 51 per cent of the variance' — an extremely strong relationship by the standards of the social sciences.

It short, the notion that illegitimate births are a general phenomenon, that young career women and girls from middle-class homes are doing it just as much as anyone else, is flatly at odds with the facts. There has been a *proportional* increase in illegitimate births among all communities, but the *prevalence* of illegitimate births is drastically higher among the lower-class communities than among the upper-class ones.

Neighbourhoods

The data I have just described are based on municipal districts. The picture gets worse when we move down to the level of the neighbourhood, though precise numbers are hard to come by. The proportion of illegitimate children in a specific poor neighbourhood can be in the vicinity not of 25 per cent, nor even of 40 per cent, but a hefty majority. And in this concentration of illegitimate births lies a generational catastrophe. Illegitimacy produces an underclass for one compelling practical reason having nothing to do with morality or the sanctity of marriage. Namely: communities need families. Communities need fathers.

This is not an argument that many intellectuals in Britain are ready to accept. I found that discussing the issue was like being in a time warp, hearing in 1989 the same rationalisations about illegitimacy that American experts used in the 1970s and early 1980s.

'Children from single-parent households do just as well as children from two-parent households.'

For example, there is the case of the National Child Development Study (NCDS), a longitudinal sample that researchers have been following since 1968. The differences between children from one-parent families and two-parent families are due to social and financial circumstances, not to the parental situation, proclaims a set of studies in *Growing Up in Great Britain*, prepared under the auspices of the National Children's Bureau.

Assessing these conclusions is made difficult by technical problems with the way that 'single-parent' and 'two-parent' families were defined (for example, a child could be defined as coming from a one-parent family if he had ever been without two parents, even briefly). But the generic problem with such analyses, and these in particular, is that all forms of single-parenthood tend to be lumped together, as if it makes no difference whether the mother is a widow, a middle-aged woman divorced after years of marriage, or a girl of 20 who has never married. All are 'single parents', and all single-parent situations are equal. I am asserting something very different: one particular form of single-parenthood — illegitimacy — constitutes a special problem for society. Single-parent situations are radically unequal.

The change in the received wisdom on this topic in the US has been remarkable. One example will serve to illustrate. In 1983, a statistic cited everywhere by those who would debunk the reactionaries was that 50 per cent of all US welfare mothers were off the welfare rolls within two years. The idea of 'welfare dependency' was a myth. Then, in 1986, David Ellwood, the scholar whose work had popularised the 50 per cent statistic, took a closer look at the same data (a large longitudinal study), separating welfare mothers into different categories. It turned out that one factor made a huge difference how quickly a woman left welfare: whether she had been married. The short-term welfare recipients were concentrated among those who had found themselves on welfare after a divorce. For the never-married woman, the average number of years on welfare was not the highly touted 2 years, but 9.3. What the people who live in Harlem and the South Bronx had known for years was finally discovered by social science: long-term welfare dependency is a fact, not a myth, among young women who have children without husbands. A similar shift in the received wisdom is occurring in research on delinquency, education, emotional development and health. Just as the scholarly mainstream has had to confront the reality of an underclass, researchers are asking new and better questions of the data about marital status, and getting more accurate answers. Even after economic circumstances are matched, the children of single mothers do worse, often much worse, than the children of married couples.

'Mainly a black problem'?

'It's mainly a black problem'. I heard this everywhere, from political clubs in Westminster to some quite sophisticated demographers in the statistical research offices. The statement is correct in this one, very limited sense: blacks born in the West Indies have much higher illegitimacy ratios — about 48 per cent of live births in the latest numbers — than all whites. But blacks constitute such a tiny proportion of the British population that their contribution to the overall illegitimacy ratio is minuscule. If there had been no blacks whatsoever in Britain (and I am including all blacks in Britain in this statement, not just those who were born abroad), the overall British illegitimacy ratio in 1988 would have dropped by about one percentage point, from 25 per cent to about 24 per cent. Blacks are not causing Britain's illegitimacy problem.

In passing, it is worth adding that the overall effect of ethnic minorities living in the UK is to *reduce* the size of the illegitimacy ratio. The Chinese, Indians, Pakistanis, Arabs and East Africans in Britain have illegitimacy ratios that are tiny compared with those of British whites.

'It's not as bad as it looks.'

In the United States, the line used to be that blacks have extended families, with uncles and grandfathers compensating for the lack of a father. In Britain, the counterpart to this cheery optimism is that an increasing number of illegitimate births are jointly registered and that an increasing number of such children are born to people who live together at the time of birth. Both joint registration and living together are quickly called evidence of 'a stable relationship'.

The statements about joint registration and living together are factually correct. Of the 158,500 illegitimate births in England and Wales in 1987, 69 per cent were jointly registered. Of those who jointly registered the birth, 70 per cent gave the same address, suggesting some kind of continuing relationship. Both of these figures have increased — in 1961, for example, only 38 per cent of illegitimate births were jointly registered, suggesting that the nature of illegitimacy in the United Kingdom has changed dramatically.

You may make what you wish of such figures. In the United States, we have stopped talking blithely about the 'extended family' in black culture that would make everything okay. It hasn't. And as the years go on, the extended family argument becomes a cruel joke — for without marriage, grandfathers and uncles too become scarce. In Britain, is it justified to assume that jointly registering a birth, or living together at the time of the birth, means a relationship that is just as stable (or nearly as stable) as a marriage? I pose it as a question because I don't have the empirical answer. But neither did any of the people who kept repeating the joint-registration and living-together numbers so optimistically.

If we can be reasonably confident that the children of never-married women do considerably worse than their peers, it remains to explain why. Progress has been slow. Until recently in the United States, scholars were reluctant to concede that illegitimacy is a legitimate variable for study. Even as that situation changes, they remain slow to leave behind their equations and go out to talk with people who are trying to raise their children in neighbourhoods with high illegitimacy rates. This is how I make sense of the combination of quantitative studies, ethnographic studies and talking-to-folks journalism that bear on the question of illegitimacy, pulling in a few observations from my conversations in Britain.

Clichés about Role Models are True

It turns out that the clichés about role models are true. Children grow up making sense of the world around them in terms of their own experience. Little boys don't naturally grow up to be responsible fathers and husbands. They don't naturally grow up knowing how to get up every morning at the same time and go to work. They don't naturally grow up thinking that work is not just a way to make money, but a way to hold one's head high in the world. And most emphatically of all, little boys do not reach adolescence naturally wanting to refrain from sex, just as little girls don't become adolescents naturally wanting to refrain from having babies. In all these ways and many more, boys and girls grow into responsible parents and neighbours and workers because they are imitating the adults around them.

That's why single-parenthood is a problem for communities, and that's why illegitimacy is the most worrisome aspect of single-parenthood. Children tend to behave like the adults around them. A child with a mother and no father, living in a neighbourhood of mothers with no fathers, judges by what he sees. You can send in social workers and school teachers and clergy to tell a young male that when he grows up he should be a good father to his children, but he doesn't know what that means unless he's seen it. Fifteen years ago, there was hardly a poor neighbourhood in urban Britain where children did not still see plentiful examples of good fathers around them. Today, the balance has already shifted in many poor neighbourhoods. In a few years, the situation will be much worse, for this is a problem that nurtures itself.

Child-Rearing in Single-Parent Communities

Hardly any of this gets into the public dialogue. In the standard newspaper or television story on single-parenthood, the reporter tracks down a struggling single parent and reports her efforts to raise her children under difficult circumstances, ending with an indictment of a stingy social system that doesn't give her enough to get along. The ignored story is what it's like for the two-parent families trying to raise their children in neighbourhoods where they now represent the exception, not the rule. Some of the problems may seem trivial but must be painfully poignant to anyone who is a parent. Take, for example, the story told me by a father who lives in such a neighbourhood in Birkenhead, near Liverpool, about the time he went to his little girl's Christmas play at school. He was the only father there — hardly any of the other children had fathers — and his daughter, embarrassed because she was different, asked him not to come to the school anymore.

The lack of fathers is also associated with a level of physical unruliness that makes life difficult. The same Birkenhead father and his wife raised their first daughter as they were raised, to be polite and considerate — and she suffered for it. Put simply, her schoolmates weren't being raised to be polite and considerate —they weren't being 'raised' at all in some respects. We have only a small body of systematic research on child-rearing practices in contemporary low-income, single-parent communities; it's one of those unfashionable topics. But the unsystematic reports I heard in towns like Birkenhead and council estates like Easterhouse in Glasgow are consistent with the reports from inner-city Washington and New York: in communities without fathers, the kids tend to run wild. The fewer the fathers, the greater the tendency. 'Run wild' can mean such simple things as young children having no set bedtime. It can mean their being left alone in the house at night while mummy goes out. It can mean an 18-month-old toddler allowed to play in the street. And, as in the case of the couple trying to raise their children as they had been raised, it can mean children who are inordinately physical and aggressive in their relationships with other children. With their second child, the Birkenhead parents eased up on their requirements for civil behaviour, realising that their children had to be able to defend themselves against threats that the parents hadn't faced when they were children. The third child is still an infant, and the mother has made a conscious decision. 'I won't knock the aggression out of her,' she said to me. Then she paused, and added angrily, 'It's *wrong* to have to decide that.'

The Key to an Underclass

I can hear the howls of objection already — lots of families raise children who have those kinds of problems, not just poor single parents. Of course. But this is why it is important to talk to parents who have lived in both kinds of communities. Ask them whether there is any difference in child-raising between a neighbourhood composed mostly of married couples and a neighbourhood composed mostly of single mothers. In Britain as in the United States — conduct the inquiries yourself — the overwhelming response is that the difference is large and palpable. The key to an underclass is not the individual instance but a situation in which a very large proportion of an entire community lacks fathers, and this is far more common in poor communities than in rich ones.

Crime and the Underclass

Crime is the next place to look for an underclass, for several reasons. First and most obviously, the habitual criminal is the classic member of an underclass. He lives off mainstream society without participating in it. But habitual criminals are only part of the problem. Once again, the key issue in thinking about an underclass is how the community functions, and crime can devastate a community in two especially important ways. To the extent that the members of a community are victimised by crime, the community tends to become fragmented. To the extent that many people in a community engage in crime as a matter of course, all sorts of the socialising norms of the community change, from the kind of men that the younger boys choose as heroes to the standards of morality in general.

Consider first the official crime figures, reported annually for England by the Home Office. As in the case of illegitimacy, I took for granted before I began this exploration that England had much lower crime rates than the United States. It therefore came as a shock to discover that England and Wales (which I will subsequently refer to as England) have a combined property crime rate apparently as high, and probably higher, than that of the United States. (I did not compare rates with Scotland and Northern Ireland, which are reported separately.) I say 'apparently' because Britain and the United States use somewhat different definitions of property crime. But burglaries, which are similarly defined in both countries, provide an example. In 1988, England had 1,623 reported burglaries per 100,000 population compared with 1,309 in the US. Adjusting for the transatlantic differences in definitions, England also appears to have had higher rates of motor vehicle theft than the United States. The rates for other kind of theft seem to have been roughly the same. I wasn't the only one who was surprised at these comparisons. I found that if you want to attract startled and incredulous attention in England, mention casually that England has a higher property crime rate than that notorious crime centre of the western world, the United States. No one will believe you.

Violent Crime

The understandable reason why they don't believe you is that *violent* crime in England remains much lower than violent crime in the United States, and it is violent crime that engenders most anxiety and anger. In this regard, Britain still lags far behind the US. This is most conspicuously true for the most violent of all crimes, homicide. In all of 1988, England and Wales recorded just 624 homicides. The United States averaged that many every 11 days — 20,675 for the year.

That's the good news. The bad news is that the violent crime rate in England and Wales has been rising very rapidly, as shown in Figure 2.

The size of the increase isn't as bad as it first looks, because England began with such a small initial rate (it's easy to double your money if you start with only a few pence — of which, more in a moment). Still, the rise is steep, and it became much steeper in about 1968. Compare the gradual increase from 1955 to 1968 with what happened subsequently. By 1988, England had 314 violent crimes reported per 100,000 people. The really bad news is that you have been experiencing this increase despite demographic trends that should have been working to your advantage. This point is important enough to explain at greater length.

The most frequent offenders, the ones who puff up the violent crime statistics, are males in the second half of their teens. As males get older, they tend to become more civilised. In both England and the United States, the number of males in this troublesome age group increased throughout the 1970s, and this fact was widely used as an explanation for increasing crime. But since the early 1980s, the size of the young male cohort has been decreasing in both countries. In the United Kingdom, for example, the number of males aged 15 to 19 hit its peak in 1982 and has subsequently decreased both as a percentage of the population and in raw numbers (by a little more than 11 per cent in both cases). Ergo, the violent crime rate 'should' have decreased as well. But it didn't. Despite the reduction in the number of males in the highest-offending age group after 1982, the violent crime rate in England from 1982 to 1988 rose by 43 per cent.

Here I must stop and briefly acknowledge a few of the many ways in which people will object that the official crime rates don't mean anything — but only briefly, because this way lies a statistical abyss.

The Significance of Official Crime Rates

One common objection is that the increase in the crime rate reflects economic growth (because there are more things to steal, especially cars and the things in the them) rather than any real change in criminal behaviour. If so, one has to ask why England enjoyed a steady decline in crime through the last half of the 19th century, when economic growth was explosive. But, to avoid argument, let us acknowledge that economic growth does make interpreting the changes in the property crime rate tricky, and focus instead on violent crime, which is not so directly facilitated by economic growth.

Another common objection is that the increase in crime is a mirage. One version of this is that crime just seems to be higher because more crimes are being reported to the police than before (because of greater access to telephones, for example, or because of the greater prevalence of insurance). The brief answer here is that it works both ways. Rape and sexual assault are more likely to be reported now, because of changes in public attitudes and judicial procedures regarding those crimes. An anonymous purse-snatch is less likely to be reported, because the victim doesn't think it will do any good. The aggregate effect of a high crime rate can be to reduce reporting, and this is most true of poor neighbourhoods where attitudes toward the police are ambiguous.

The most outrageously spurious version of the 'crime isn't really getting worse' argument uses *rate* of increase rather than the *magnitude* of increase to make the case. The best example in Britain is the argument that public concern about muggings in the early 1970s was simply an effort to scapegoat young blacks, and resulted in a 'moral panic'. The sociologist Stuart Hall and his colleagues made this case at some length in a book entitled *Policing the Crisis*,[1] in which, among other things, they blithely argued that because the rate of increase in violent crimes was decreasing, the public's concern was unwarranted. It is the familiar problem of low baselines. From 1950 to 1958, violent crime in England rose by 88 per cent (the crime rate began at 14 crimes per 100,000 persons and rose by 13). From 1980 to 1988, violent crime in England rose by only 60 per cent (it began at 196 crimes per 100,000 persons and rose by 118). In other words, by the logic of Hall and his colleagues, things are getting much better, because the rate of increase in the 1980s has been lower than it was during the comparable period of the 1950s. Now take another look at the graph of violent crime. Is everyone convinced?

The Intellectual Conventional Wisdom

The denial by intellectuals that crime really has been getting worse spills over into denial that poor communities are more violent places than affluent communities. To the people who live in poor communities, this doesn't make much sense. One man in a poor, high-crime community told me about his experience in an open university where he had decided to try to improve himself.

---

[1] London: Macmillan, 1978.

He took a sociology course about poverty. The professor kept talking about this 'nice little world that the poor live in', the man remembered. The professor scoffed at the reactionary myth that poor communities are violent places. To the man who lived in such a community, it was 'bloody drivel'. A few weeks later, a class exercise called for the students to canvass a poor neighbourhood. The professor went along, but apparently he, too, suspected that some of this pronouncements were bloody drivel — he cautiously stayed in his car and declined to knock on doors himself. And that raises the most interesting question regarding the view that crime has not risen, or that crime is not especially a problem in lower-class communities: do any of the people who hold this view actually *believe* it, to the extent that they take no more precautions walking in a slum neighbourhood than they do in a middle-class suburb?

These comments will not still the battle over the numbers. But I will venture this prediction, once again drawn from the American experience. After a few more years, quietly and without anyone having to admit he had been wrong, the intellectual conventional wisdom in Britain as in the United States will undergo a gradual transition. After all the statistical artifacts are taken into account and argued over, it will be decided that England is indeed becoming a more dangerous place in which to live: that this unhappy process is not occurring everywhere, but disproportionately in particular types of neighbourhoods; and that those neighbourhoods turn out to be the ones in which an underclass is taking over. Reality will once again force theory to its knees.

Unemployment and the Underclass

If illegitimate births are the leading indicator of an underclass and violent crime a proxy measure of its development, the definitive proof that an underclass has arrived is that large numbers of young, healthy, low-income males choose not to take jobs. (The young idle rich are a separate problem.) This decrease in labour force participation is the most elusive of the trends in the growth of the British underclass.

The main barrier to understanding what's going on is the high unemployment of the 1980s. The official statistics distinguish between 'unemployed' and 'economically inactive', but Britain's unemployment figures (like those in the US) include an unknown but probably considerable number of people who manage to qualify for benefit even if in reality very few job opportunities would tempt them to work.

On the other side of the ledger, over a prolonged period of high unemployment the 'economically inactive' category includes men who would like to work but have given up. To make matters still more complicated, there is the 'black economy' to consider, in which people who are listed as 'economically inactive' are really working for cash, not reporting their income to the authorities. So we are looking through a glass darkly, and I have more questions than answers.

Economic Inactivity and Social Class

The simple relationship of economic inactivity to social class is strong, just as it was for illegitimacy. According to the 1981 census data, the municipal districts with high proportions of household heads who are in Class V (unskilled labour) also tend to have the highest levels of 'economically inactive' persons of working age (statistically, the proportion of Class V households explains more than a third of the variance when inactivity because of retirement is taken into account).

This is another way of saying that you will find many more working-aged people who are neither working nor looking for work in the slums than in the suburbs. Some of these persons are undoubtedly discouraged workers, but two questions need to be asked and answered with far more data than are currently available — specifically, questions about lower-class young males.

Lower-Class Young Males

First, after taking into account Britain's unemployment problems when the 1981 census was taken, were the levels of economic inactivity among young males consistent with the behaviour of their older brothers and fathers during earlier periods? Or were they dropping out more quickly and often than earlier cohorts of young men?

Second, Britain has for the past few years been conducting a natural experiment, with an economic boom in the south and high unemployment in the north. If lack of jobs is the problem, then presumably economic inactivity among lower-class healthy young males in the south has plummeted to insignificant levels. Has it?

The theme that I heard from a variety of people in Birkenhead and Easterhouse was that the youths who came of age in the late 1970s are in danger of being a lost generation. All of them did indeed ascribe the problem to the surge in unemployment at the end of the 1970s. 'They came out of school at the wrong time,' as one older resident of Easterhouse put it, and have never in their lives held a real job. They are now in their late twenties. As economic times improve, they are competing for the same entry-level jobs as people 10 years younger, and employers prefer to hire the youngsters. But it's more complicated than that, he added. 'They've lost the picture of what they're going to be doing.' When he was growing up, he could see himself in his father's job. Not these young men.

The Generation Gap

This generation gap was portrayed to me as being only a few years wide. A man from Birkenhead in his early thirties who had worked steadily from the time he left school until 1979, when he lost his job as an assembly-line worker, recalled how the humiliation and desperation to work remained even as his unemployment stretched from months into years. He — and the others in their thirties and forties and fifties — were the ones showing up at six in the morning when jobs were advertised. They were the ones who sought jobs even if they paid less than the benefit rate.

'The only income I wanted was enough to be free of the bloody benefit system,' he said. 'It was like a rope around my neck.' The phrase for being on benefit that some of them used, 'on the suck', says a great deal about how little they like their situation.

This attitude is no small asset to Britain. In some inner cities of the US, the slang for robbing someone is 'getting paid'. Compare that inversion of values with the values implied by 'on the suck'. Britain in 1989 has resources that make predicting the course of the underclass on the basis of the US experience very dicey.

But the same men who talk this way often have little in common with their sons and younger brothers. Talking to the boys in their late teens and early twenties about jobs, I heard nothing about the importance of work as a source of self-respect and no talk of just wanting enough income to be free of the benefit system. To make a decent living, a youth of 21 explained to me, you need £200 a week — after taxes. He would accept less if it was all he could get. But he conveyed clearly that he would feel exploited. As for the Government's employment training scheme, YTS, that's 'slave labour'. Why, another young man asked me indignantly, should he and his friends be deprived of their right to a full unemployment benefit just because they haven't reached 18 yet? It sounded strange to my ears — a 'right' to unemployment benefit for a school-age minor who's never held a job. But there is no question in any of their minds that that's exactly what the unemployment benefit is: a right, in every sense of the word. The boys did not mention what they considered to be their part of the bargain.

'I was brought up thinking work is something you are morally obliged to do,' as one older man put it. With the younger generation, he said, 'that culture isn't going to be there at all.' And there are anecdotes to go with these observations. For example, the contractors carrying out the extensive housing refurbishment now going on at Easterhouse are obliged to hire local youths for unskilled labour as part of a work-experience scheme. Thirty Easterhouse young men applied for a recent set of openings. Thirteen were accepted. Ten actually came to work the first day. By the end of the first week, only one was still showing up.

A Generation Gap by Class

My hypothesis — the evidence is too fragmentary to call it more than that — is that Britain is experiencing a generation gap by class. Well-educated young people from affluent homes are working in larger proportions and working longer hours than ever. The attitudes and behaviour of the middle-aged working class haven't changed much. The change in stance toward the labour force is concentrated among lower-class young men in their teens and twenties. It is not a huge change. I am not suggesting that a third or a quarter or even a fifth of lower-class young people are indifferent to work. An underclass doesn't have to be huge to become a problem.

That problem is remarkably difficult to fix. It seems simple — just make decent-paying jobs available. But it doesn't work that way. In the States, we've tried nearly everything — training programmes, guaranteed jobs, special 'socialisation' programmes that taught not only job skills but also 'work-readiness skills' such as getting to work on time, 'buddy' systems whereby an experienced older man tried to ease the trainee into the world of work. The results of these strategies, carefully evaluated against control groups, have consistently showed little effect at best, no effect most commonly, and occasionally negative effects.

If this seems too pessimistic for British youth, the Government or some private foundation may easily try this experiment: go down to the Bull Ring near Waterloo Bridge where one of London's largest cardboard cities is located. Pass over the young men who are alcoholics or drug addicts or mentally disturbed, selecting only those who seem clear-headed (there are many). Then offer them jobs at a generous wage for unskilled labour and see what happens. Add in a training component if you wish. Or, if you sympathise with their lack of interest in unskilled jobs, offer them more extensive training that would qualify them for skilled jobs. Carry out your promises to them, spend as much as you wish, and measure the results after 2 years against the experience of similar youths who received no such help. I am betting that you, too, will find 'no effect'. It is an irretrievable disaster for young men to grow up without being socialised into the world of work.

Work is at the Centre of Life

The reason why it is a disaster is not that these young men cause upright taxpayers to spend too much money supporting them. That is a nuisance. The disaster is to the young men themselves and the communities in which they live. Looking around the inner cities of the United States, a view which has been eloquently voiced in the past by people as disparate as Thomas Carlyle and Karl Marx seems increasingly validated by events: work is at the centre of life. By remaining out of the work force during the crucial formative years, young men aren't just losing a few years of job experience. They are missing out on the time in which they need to have been acquiring the skills and the networks of friends and experiences that enable them to establish a place for themselves — not only in the workplace, but a vantage point from which they can make sense of themselves and their lives.

Furthermore, when large numbers of young men don't work, the communities around them break down, just as they break down when large numbers of young unmarried women have babies. The two phenomena are intimately related. Just as work is more important than merely making a living, getting married and raising a family are more than a way to pass the time. Supporting a family is a central means for a man to prove to himself that he is a 'mensch'. Men who do not support families find other ways to prove that they are men, which tend to take various destructive forms. As many have commented through the centuries, young males are essentially barbarians for whom marriage — meaning not just the wedding vows, but the act of taking responsibility for a wife and children — is an indispensable civilising force. Young men who don't work don't make good marriage material. Often they don't get married at all; when they do, they haven't the ability to fill their traditional role. In either case, too many of them remain barbarians.

The Size of the British Underclass

How big is the British underclass? It all depends on how one defines its membership; trying to take a headcount is a waste of time. The size of the underclass can be made to look huge or insignificant, depending on what one wants the answer to be.

But it seems safe to conclude that as of 1989 the British underclass is still small enough not to represent nearly the problem that it does in the US. If the crime and illegitimacy trends in Britain magically level off where they are now and then the tight labour market that the south now enjoys spreads to the north, Britain would continue to have an underclass but not one that would force major reform. Britain could continue to treat social policy as it has since the Beveridge Report of 1942, looking for ways to fine-tune a social welfare and criminal justice system that most Britons think works pretty well.

The question facing Britain is the same, haunting question facing the United States: how contagious is this disease? Is it going to spread indefinitely, or will it be self-containing?

Suppose, for example, that the trends continue unabated, and try to imagine Britain 10 years from now. The results seem preposterous. If violent crime follows the steepening trendline it has displayed since 1969, by 1999 your violent crime rate will be double the rate that already is a source of such concern. In the case of illegitimacy, it is impossible to assume that the exponential curve in the trendline since 1970 will continue to steepen — if it were to do so, all British births would be illegitimate by the end of the century. But even if we assume more conservatively that the trend of the past 10 years will

24

continue linearly, more than 40 per cent of births will be to single women by 1999. Because these results are so obviously preposterous, the question arises: why might these projections be too high? Why may we reasonably expect that recent trends are caused by abnormal forces that are about to fade?

Questions about causation

Here we reach controversial questions about causation. Frank Field, in his book on the emergence of a British underclass, *Losing Out*,[1] has no difficulty laying the blame at Mrs Thatcher's door. The organising principle for Field's analysis is inequality. The Thatcherites have rewarded the rich and punished the poor, increased inequalities, and hence (I am greatly simplifying an argument worth reading) Britain has a growing underclass. Change the policies, and the underclass will diminish.

My interpretation and those of the Left do not so much compete as pass in the night. As far as I can tell, inequality in general and Mrs Thatcher's policies in particular hardly enter in. The increases in crime extend back to the 1950s, and the slope in the graph in violent crime steepened most conspicuously in the late 1960s, long before Mrs Thatcher came to power. The acceleration in the illegitimacy ratio was taking off in 1979, and was as nearly as steep as it would ever get by Mrs Thatcher's first full year in office. It is hard to credit that Mrs Thatcher's influence on fertility behaviour among single young women occurred within days of her election.

In any case, let me propose a more radical reason why the Thatcher Government's policies have little to do with the development of an underclass: the relevant policies haven't changed that much under Mrs Thatcher. Despite the many dramatic changes in Britain in other spheres, the culprits behind the trends I have described have been largely unaffected.

[1] London: Blackwell, 1989.

I am recasting a version of the Right's view of why things go wrong that is usually expressed in terms of the decay of moral standards, the perverse incentives of welfare policy and the coddling of criminals. The problem with those arguments as they are usually presented is that they are too mechanistic. I do not believe women read about the latest change in the benefit rules for unwed mothers and use a pocket calculator to decide whether to get pregnant, or that young men decide whether to rob the local building society on the basis of a favourable change in parole policy.

Let us think instead in more common-sense terms. The topic is young people in their late teens and early twenties. The proposition is as simple as this: young people — not just poor young people, but all young people — try to make sense of the world around them. They behave in ways that reflect what they observe. In the 1960s and 1970s social policy in Britain fundamentally changed what makes sense. The changes did not affect the mature as much as the young. They affected the affluent hardly at all. Rather: the rules of the game changed fundamentally for low-income young people. Behaviour changed along with the changes in the rules.

'Making sense of the world around them' has to be understood in terms of the judgement and the time frame of the young person. Late adolescence is a critical time of life for shaping the future, and unfortunately also a time during which people are prone to do things that are foolish and self-destructive in the long term.

Crime Has Become Safer

Consider how the world was changing at the time when the trendlines in crime and illegitimacy were changing. I begin with crime, assuming this common-sense view of the situation: if the chances that one will get punished for a crime go down, then crime goes up. In every respect — the chances of getting caught, the chances of being found guilty and the chances of going to prison — crime has become dramatically safer in Britain through-out the post-war period, and most blatantly safer since 1960.

Clear-up rates provide an example. With a few crimes such as homicide, the clear-up rate has remained high and unchanged. But for a crime such as robbery, the clear-up rate has fallen from 61 per cent in 1960 to 21 per cent in 1987 — an extremely large change. Reductions for other crimes have been smaller but significant.

If clear-up rates had been the only thing to change, then the overall effect on the 'safeness' of crime would have been modest. But at the same time as clear-up rates were falling, so was the likelihood that one would be convicted for a crime even if caught. In 1960, 50 per cent of all cleared-up offenses resulted in a conviction. By 1987, this proportion had fallen to 30 per cent.

Perhaps most importantly, the penalties imposed upon those convicted changed. This last topic is a source of great misun-derstanding, for prison is the most obvious form of punishment and prisons are commonly accepted to be useless for reducing crime. Partly, the misunderstanding arises from a confusion between the limitations of prisons in rehabilitating people (which is reasonably well-documented) and the nature of the deterrent effect of prisons on potential offenders (which is not). Strict and consistent use of prisons, as once characterised Britain, can at the same time be miserably inefficient at rehabilitating criminals and spectacularly effective in deterring people from becoming criminals in the first place.

Another misunderstanding lies in the tendency of people to think in terms of the raw number of people in prison. As the number of prisoners rises but crime also continues to rise, the conclusion is loudly proclaimed that it doesn't do any good to incarcerate people. But if one is thinking in terms of risks, the obvious measure is not the number of people in prison, but rather the chances of going to prison if one commits a crime. That figure has plummeted. Prison sentences as a proportion of reported crimes fell by half during the period 1950 to 1970, and the 1970 figure had fallen again by half by 1987.

But comparatively few offenders were sent to prison even in the tough old days. This statistic may be treated as an example, not the whole story. 'Penalty' doesn't mean simply 'prison', nor even 'the judge's sentence'. Swiftness, certainty, consistency, and comparative severity of penalties are also important. A full analysis of the trends in punishment would consider fines as well as prison sentences; the use of cautions and suspended sentences; the effects of the parole system on actual time served; the delay between arrest and disposition; and a host of other factors that affect how a person arrested for a given crime in 1950 was treated differently from a person arrested for the same offence today. It seems evident from descriptions in the press and essays on the criminal justice system that the use of penalties has fallen in every dimension — not just severity, but swiftness and certainty, too.

The Use of Penalties has fallen

Even using simple measures, recent trends in penalties are at odds with the reputation of the Thatcher Government as tough, anti-crime and punitive. From 1982 to 1987, even as crime continued to rise, the number of convictions and prison sentences dropped — not just as a proportion of crimes, but in raw numbers. In 1982, 3.3 million indictable offences were known to the police, 475,000 persons were found guilty of them; of these, 50,300 received unsuspended prison sentences. In 1987, 3.9 million indictable offences were known to the police (up to 19 per cent), 386,000 were found guilty of them (down 19 per cent); of these, 41,700 received unsuspended prison sentences (down 17 per cent). People who use the past few years as evidence that a 'get rough' policy doesn't work aren't defining 'get tough' from the criminal's point of view.

Because crime statistics are so subject to qualifications (including the ones just presented — some form of 'immediate custody' for violent crimes went up during this period, for example) and punishment itself is a subject of such great passion, let me make clear what I am and am not saying. I'm not claiming that the police have become lax (they've been overwhelmed), nor that one must ignore the complicated social forces associated with increases in crime. Just this: committing a crime has been getting safer for more than three decades, and the trend continues today. That being the case, why shouldn't crime continue to increase? In fact, why shouldn't the slope in the graph of violent crime continue just as steeply upwards for the next 10 years? It might flatten out, but it is difficult to think of a good reason why.

Similarly, why shouldn't illegitimacy continue to increase? There is an obvious explanation for why single young women get pregnant: sex is fun and babies endearing. Nothing could be more natural than for young men and women to want to have sex, and nothing could be more natural than for a young woman to want a baby. A better question than asking why single young women get pregnant is to ask why they don't. The obvious answer is that in the past it was very punishing for a single woman to have a baby. (If that seems too negative, then one may say that a young single woman who had a baby had to forego many social and economic rewards.)

Social Stigma and Illegitimacy

One type of punishment was social stigma (or one type of reward for virtue was social acceptance), and without doubt the sexual revolution of the 1960s markedly reduced the stigma. Leaving aside the subtle question of why this happened, it is reasonable to expect that illegitimacy would have risen in the 1960s even if social policy had remained unchanged. But in addition to stigma, there was, historically, severe economic punishment awaiting single mothers. For a poor single woman, supporting a baby alone was next to impossible. Getting into that situation was something actively to be avoided.

The Benefit System

At this point we come to the benefit system, and another source of great controversy and confusion. Conservatives in particular often misconstrue the problem, railing against the woman who goes out and gets pregnant so that she can get on the dole. It happens occasionally but, as far as anyone knows, the reason why single young women have babies is seldom specifically so that they can get income benefits. (Sometimes they have a second child specifically so that they can *remain* on benefit, but that constitutes a comparatively minor part of the problem.)

Rather, the problem in providing money to single women is that the income enables many young women to do something they would naturally like to do. Such benefits don't have much effect on affluent women — the benefit rate is so far below what they consider their needs, that they are not in any way 'enabled' to have babies by the level of support being provided. For poor women, however, the benefit level can be quite salient in deciding whether having a baby is feasible. And the simple economic feasibility of raising a baby without the support of a father has changed fundamentally since the end of the Second World War.

In 1955, for example, an unmarried, unemployed mother with a single child under five had to get along on less than £22 a week in 1987 purchasing power, miserably little. It was almost impossible to survive on such a budget. Unless the mother had some other source of support, the only realistic option was putting the child up for adoption or into the care of the local authority. Having an illegitimate baby was brutally punishing if you were poor. (It was also punishing if you were rich, but for different reasons.) During the 1960s the benefit grew, reaching about £36 in 1987 purchasing power by 1970 — still a slender stipend, though conceivably enough to get by on.

The Homeless Persons Act

During the first half of the 1970s the size of the benefit for single women began to rise more rapidly, increasing more than a third in purchasing power from 1970 to 1976. Then, in 1977, the Homeless Persons Act was passed. Before, a single mother had to wait in a queue for housing, but the new act stipulated that pregnant women and single mothers must get some sort of housing immediately — and go to the top of the queue for council housing — if they could demonstrate to the local authority's satisfaction that they couldn't live with their parents and were otherwise homeless.

I doubt that the Homeless Persons Act bribed many young women to have babies so that they could get their own flats. Rather, the increases in the benefits and the Homeless Persons Act were steps in a quiet, commonsensical, cumulative process whereby having a baby as a single mother went from 'extremely punishing' to 'not so bad'. By 1977, poor young women looking at the world around them could see that single mothers in their neighbourhoods were getting along, whereas a similar young woman in the 1950s would have looked around and concluded that single motherhood was an awful state to be in. The combination of cash and housing was not a package large enough to appeal to the middle class, but for a low-income young woman it provided a standard of living no worse and often better than she endured living with her parents. Meanwhile, sex was as fun as ever and babies were as endearing as ever. By the end of 1978 (one is tempted to add, beginning within the next nine months), the illegitimacy ratio had begun the rapid rise that has continued throughout the 1980s.

Once again, on this most inflammatory issue, let me be explicit about what I'm *not* saying. I'm not saying that single young women get pregnant for the money. I'm not chiding them for immorality. I'm not saying that they don't love their babies. I'm not saying that a 10 per cent cut in benefits will mean a 10 per cent reduction (or any reduction) in fertility among single women. Rather, a series of changes in the benefit rates and collateral housing benefits lifted a large portion of low-income young women above the threshold where having and keeping a baby became economically feasible.

It doesn't make any difference if the benefit level stops getting higher, or even if it diminishes somewhat. As long as the benefit level is well above the threshold, the dynamics of social incentives will continue to work in favour of illegitimacy as over time the advantages of legal marriage become less clear and its disadvantages more obvious. For men, the pressures to marry will continue to diminish. Given all this, I cannot see why the illegitimacy ratio should start to level off. It hasn't done so among poor people in the United States, where the illegitimacy ratio among blacks is now over 60 per cent. Why should poor whites in Britain be any different?

Social Problems are Interconnected

These changes in the law enforcement and benefit systems are not occurring in isolation. State education was a lively topic of conversation among people with whom I talked everywhere: the stories sounded depressingly like the problems with urban public education in the United States. Drug abuse in Britain is reported to be increasing significantly. Everything interacts. When one leaves school without any job skills, barely literate, the job alternatives to crime or having a baby or the dole are not attractive. Young men who are subsisting in crime or the dole are not likely to be trustworthy providers, which makes having a baby without a husband a more practical alternative. If a young man's girl friend doesn't need him to help support the baby, it makes less sense for him to plug away at a menial job and more sense to have some fun — which in turn makes hustling and crime more attractive, marriage less attractive. Without a job or family to give life meaning, drugs become that much more valuable as a means of distraction. The cost of drugs makes crime the only feasible way to make enough money to pay for them. The interconnections go on endlessly, linking up with the reasons why community norms change, the role of older adults in the community changes, community bonds change.

Incremental Changes Won't Solve the Problem

The implication of these interconnections is that modest, incremental changes in one corner of the system are unlikely to have much effect. Everybody's pet solutions are wrong. People on the Right who think that they can reduce illegitimacy by snipping benefits are wrong. (Illegitimacy would be cut radically if you slashed benefits back to the 1970 level, but that's not under consideration.) The notion that giving the police more latitude or legislating longer prison sentences will reduce crime is wrong. (Crime would be cut radically if you enforced laws as strictly as you did in 1950, but in the short term that would mean tripling your prison population and vastly expanding your court system.)

People on the Left who think things will get better when Labour comes back to power are just as wrong. The accepted wisdom on the Left is that all this is the fault of the Thatcher Government, the soaring unemployment that began in the late 1970s, and an ethos of greed and individualism. An American familiar with the history of the 1960s in the United States is slow to buy that explanation. There, the surge in crime and illegitimacy and drop-out from the labour force coincided with the ascendency of the Left and with prosperity.

This imponderable remains: what will happen if jobs do become plentiful everywhere? In the United States, the experts are still trying to come to terms with what has become too obvious to ignore. Throughout the 1970s, the conventional wisdom on the Left was that scarcity of jobs was the root problem and the provision of jobs was the root solution. But during the past five years, several American cities have enjoyed red-hot economies, with low-skill jobs paying good wages easily available. The evidence is accumulating that this economic growth is having almost no effect on the size of the underclass. Many of the drop-outs don't even want such jobs — they are 'demeaning' because they are menial, 'chump change' even if they pay $5 or $6 an hour. Others say they want jobs, and apply for them, then stop showing up after a few days. Or they get into fights with their co-workers and supervisors and are fired, because they cannot deal with the discipline of the workplace.

Once jobs become available, will the young British males who have been shut out of the labour force come flocking back? Some will, but others won't, and, in counting them, Britain will begin to get some idea of how large the underclass has become.

What Can Britain Learn from the American Experience?

Britain is not the United States, and the most certain of predictions is that the British experience will play out differently from the US experience. At the close of this brief tour of several huge topics, I will be the first to acknowledge that I have skipped over complications and nuances and certainly missed all sorts of special British conditions of which I am ignorant. Still, so much has been the same so far. In both countries, the same humane impulses and the same intellectual fashions drove the reforms in social policy. The attempts to explain away the consequences have been similar, with British intellectuals in the 1980s saying the same things that American intellectuals were saying in the 1970s about how the problems are'nt really as bad as they seem.

So if the United States has had so much more experience with a growing underclass, what can Britain learn from it? The sad answer is — not much. The central truth that the politicians in the United States are unwilling to face is our powerlessness to deal with an underclass once it exists. No matter how much money we spend on our cleverest social interventions, we don't know how to turn around the lives of teenagers who have grown up in an underclass culture. Providing educational opportunities or job opportunities doesn't do it. Training programmes don't reach the people who need them most. We don't know how to make up for the lack of good parents — day-care doesn't do it, foster homes don't work very well. Most of all, we don't know how to make up for the lack of a community that rewards responsibility and stigmatises irresponsibility.

Let me emphasise the words: *we do not know how*. It's not money we lack, but the capability to social-engineer our way out of this situation. Unfortunately, the delusions persists that our social engineering simply hasn't been clever enough, and that we must strive to become more clever.

Authentic Self-Government is the Key

The alternative I advocate is to have the central government stop trying to be clever and instead get out of the way, giving poor communities (and affluent communities, too) a massive dose of self-government, with vastly greater responsibility for the operation of the institutions that affect their lives — including the criminal justice, educational, housing and benefit systems in their localities. My premise is that it is unnatural for a neighbourhood to tolerate high levels of crime or illegitimacy or voluntary idleness among its youth: that, given the chance, poor communities as well as rich ones will run affairs so that such things happen infrequently. And when communities with different values run their affairs differently, I want to make it as easy as possible for people who share values to live together. If people in one neighbourhood think marriage is an outmoded institution, fine; let them run their neighbourhood as they see fit. But make it easy for the couple who thinks otherwise to move into a neighbourhood where two-parent families are valued. There are many ways that current levels of expenditure for public systems could be sustained (if that is thought to be necessary) but control over them decentralised. Money isn't the key. Authentic self-government is.

But this is a radical solution, and the explanation of why it might work took me 300 pages the last time I tried. In any case, no one in either the United States or Britain is seriously contemplating such steps. That leaves both countries with similar arsenals of social programmes which don't work very well, and the prospect of an underclass in both countries that not only continues but grows.

Oddly, this does not necessarily mean that the pressure for major reforms will increase. It is fairly easy to propitiate the consciences of the well-off and pacify rebellion among the poor with a combination of benefits and social programmes that at least employ large numbers of social service professionals. Such is the strategy that the United States has willy-nilly adopted. Even if the underclass is out there and still growing, it needn't bother the rest of us too much as long as it stays in its own part of town. Everybody's happy — or at least not so unhappy that more action has to be taken.

The Bleak Message

So, Britain, that's the bleak message. Not only do you have an underclass, not only is it growing, but, judging from the American experience, there's not much in either the Conservative or Labour agendas that has a chance of doing anything about it. A few years ago I wrote for an American audience that the real contest about social policy is not between people who want to cut budgets and people who want to help. Watching Britain replay our history, I can do no better than repeat the same conclusion. When meaningful reforms finally do occur, they will happen not because stingy people have won, but because generous people have stopped kidding themselves.

Figure 1
Births to Single Women as a Percentage of All Births

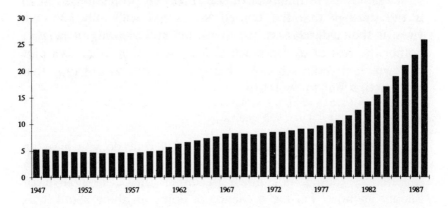

Figure 2
Crimes of Violence per 100,000 Population

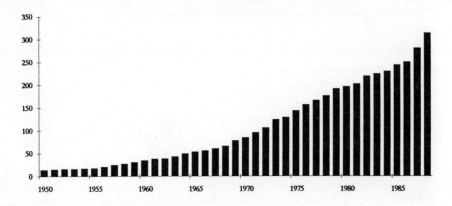

2

BRITAIN'S UNDERCLASS:
COUNTERING THE GROWTH

Frank Field MP

Charles Murray's work illustrates both the advantage and disadvantage of looking in at somebody else's country. His advantage is to bring a new pair of eyes when examining a social landscape of which others have become tired of describing. But the fresh pair of eyes have been trained to look at the American terrain and so there is the danger of trying to transpose an American vision onto Britain.

Some commentators will no doubt have fun in writing good knocking copy against Murray's view. His errors of fact, or unusualness of interpretation, should not blind anyone to Murray's main message. He seeks to show that something new is happening in Britain and that an underclass is emerging here as assuredly as it is prominent in American society.

As I have attempted to set out in *Losing Out: the Emergence of Britain's Underclass*, I accept that Britain does now have a group of poor people who are so distinguished from others on low income that it is appropriate to use the term 'underclass' to describe their position in the social hierarchy.[1]

---

[1] London: Blackwell, 1989.

A Racial Phenomenon

It is, however, necessary at the outset to distinguish a fundamental difference between British and American society. The difference is clearly expressed in Nicholas Lemann's influential contribution to the American debate. Writing in the *Atlantic Monthly* he portrays an underclass largely as a racial phenomenon. Lemann writes that the

> underclass did not just spring into being over the past twenty years. Every aspect of the underclass culture in the ghetto is directly traceable to roots in the South — not the South of slavery, but the South of a generation ago. In fact, there seems to be a strong correlation between the underclass status in the North, and the family background in the nascent underclass of the share-cropper South.[1]

There is no racial basis to Britain's underclass. To be sure, many blacks are to be found in its ranks, but they are there because they occupy some of the most vulnerable positions in British society. Where there are no blacks — such as in Birkenhead — the underclass is composed exclusively of poor whites.

This distinction between the two countries is also important for the prescriptive part of any debate on Britain's underclass. Too much of American literature — and Charles Murray is guilty here — employs a 'culture of poverty' interpretation of the underclass's advent. While it is important that the attitudes of the poor are considered, they do not by themselves give an adequate understanding as to why this new social phenomenon has occurred.

Structural Causes of the Underclass

In Britain it is important to begin with emphasising the structural causes of the underclass. I see this group composed of three

---

[1] June 1986, p. 35.

groups; the very frail, elderly pensioner, the single parent with no chance of escaping welfare under the existing rules and with prevailing attitudes, and the long-term unemployed.

Pensioner income has recently risen substantially. But not all pensioners have benefited from the major increases in the real value of occupational pensions. Elderly pensioners, by and large, are those without a private pension and are overwhelmingly much the poorer. This group has been particularly hard hit by the present Government's decision to break the link between state pensions and the rise in earnings or prices — taking whichever is the most favourable to pensioners. This action, which reversed the Macmillan Government's decision to tie in the living standards of those on welfare with rising prosperity, is more responsible than any other action in economically cutting this group off from other groups, and recruiting it into the underclass. No-one in their right mind believes that this group has volunteered for membership.

Single-Parent Families and the Unemployed

The position is somewhat different in respect of single-parent families and the unemployed. There is no question that the vast majority of both of these two groups initially viewed membership of the underclass with disdain. But once in the underclass, attitudes have changed. Countering the growth in the underclass amongst these two groups requires new policies and determination.

The fastest growing group on welfare is single mothers. Amongst this group, the biggest increase is now in very young single mothers. In countering this trend it is crucial that young girls in school should learn from young single mothers that having a baby does result in jumping the housing queue, but only as far as the first sink council estate. Similarly, young males need to learn that the state will hold them responsible for the maintenance of their children. Maintenance orders attached to the man's national insurance record would ensure that today's dodge — of constantly changing jobs so that the mother has to

40

go back to court for a new attachment of earnings — becomes pointless.

Full Employment UK

The pioneering work that Full Employment UK has undertaken amongst the unemployed shows how much more difficult it is going to be to encourage back into mainstream society the disillusioned young unemployed worker. Of course, in areas of high unemployment there are large numbers of people willing to take almost any job.

But that is not true in areas where the labour market is tight. Some of these unemployed young workers use the Government's Employment Training schemes merely to win more time on welfare rather than as an entry into the labour market. Many, too, have criminal records which make the prospect of gaining employment a near impossibility — unless one has an amnesty on such criminal records. Many of this group now simply despise those who are on the inside of the labour market in low-paid jobs.

Enforcing fairly an availability-for-work test is crucial so that people do take work when it is available. Without the structure that work gives to our day, many people's lives simply disintegrate. It is here, however, that the needs of the unemployed underclass, and the low paid are identical. As a policy of reinforcing the position of those who are playing by society's rules in the labour market it is crucial that training is personalised. Without this, many low-paid workers will be trapped with employers who not only pay badly but who resolutely refuse to give workers the chance of exiting from low-paid jobs by increasing their skills.

The personal approach to training will similarly be required by many of today's unemployed. Full Employment UK has advocated the introduction of personalised training accounts, the value of which is built up from the worker himself, his employer and the Government. The introduction of such accounts would make the policing of existing training programmes that much less important.

Workers, realising what a bad deal they are getting, and knowing that the course will be paid from their own training accounts, will vote with their feet and enrol in other courses.

But this assumes that both the low paid and the unemployed have a clear idea of their own skills, their potential, and likely changes in the labour market over the coming decade. The employment service needs to begin behaving as though it believed in its title. The building up of career advisers will also play a crucial part in a transformed employment service.

A Comprehensive Approach

A comprehensive approach needs to knit together other policies too. But the watershed must be that more of the same sorts of policies will do little to prevent new groups from becoming disaffected, or to change the balance of advantage in joining society for those who have already been sectioned into Britain's underclass.

3

THE FOCUS ON
SINGLE MOTHERS

Joan C. Brown

It is quite easy to put together a package of figures — all
authentic — which creates a particular kind of picture of one-
parent families, 90 per cent of whom are headed by a woman.
They form a growing proportion of all families with children, up
from 8 per cent in 1971 to 14 per cent in 1986 and 16 per cent
in 1988. The numbers have risen from 570,000 in 1971 to over
one million in 1986. The rate of births outside marriage has also
increased, from 8 per cent in 1971 to 21 per cent in 1986 and 25
per cent in 1988.

The number of lone mothers on Supplementary Benefit (now
Income Support) has gone up accordingly, from 238,000 in
November 1971 to 578,000 in February 1986. In that month,
some 93 per cent of single (never married) mothers were on SB,
95 per cent of separated mothers and 42 per cent of divorced
mothers. Single mothers were the largest single group of lone
mothers on benefit, 213,000 of them, followed by 180,000
separated wives and 172,000 divorced women. The balance were
widows and wives of prisoners.

The available figures do not support what is apparently the
assumption of some politicians, that 75 per cent of lone mothers
are single never-married mothers. Although there is a proportion-
ate increase in this group, as the number of widows has declined,
they still constitute just over one-quarter of lone mothers, the
dominant group being formerly married mothers. Nor can the

idea that this is a 'black problem' be sustained — and here I agree with Charles Murray. A recent analysis by Haskey has shown that, while the proportion of one parent families among the ethnic minority population of West Indian origin is notably higher than among the white population, West Indian families constitute only one per cent of all families in Great Britain.[1] Their influence on the one-parent family figure is, therefore, minimal.

Still, the picture the figures present is of a growing population of one-parent families, mostly fatherless families, dependent on benefits to quite a staggering extent. Moreover, while in 1986, 50 per cent of married mothers went out to work to help support their families, only 42 per cent of lone mothers worked, and as few as 25 per cent of single mothers, and half of them part time only. Such figures are often used to suggest a willingness, or even a preference to be dependent long term on state benefits, especially by single mothers.

The Misleading Nature of Statistics

But all of these statistics are point-in-time figures. They provide a snapshot of one-parent families at the end of one month in a year. Murray believes, arguing from US experience, that for single mothers, the picture is nevertheless substantially correct. But while the US did not produce figures separating welfare mothers into different categories until 1986, when single mothers were shown to spend far longer on welfare than other lone mothers, the DHSS has been publishing categorised figures for the duration spent on Supplementary Benefit going back to 1970. It is true that these do not show the sum of different spells on benefit — for example, of a lone mother who leaves benefit for work and then loses the job and has to reclaim — but the figures are, nevertheless, quite enlightening, and do not support Murray's thesis.

---

[1] John Haskey, 'Families and Households of Ethnic Minority and White Populations of Great Britain', *Population Trends*, 57, Autumn 1989, pp. 8-19.

In 1981, of those on benefit, 7.8 per cent of single mothers and 9.6 per cent of divorced mothers had been on SB for more than 10 years, and 15.6 per cent of single and 27.4 per cent of divorced mothers had been on benefit for 5-9 years, giving a 5 years plus total for 23 per cent of single mothers and 37 per cent of the divorced mothers. By 1987 (when only 5 years plus figures were published), 27 per cent of single mothers were this long on benefit and 37 per cent of divorced mothers. The duration on benefit of single mothers has increased — a trend that may in part be attributed to high unemployment in the 1980s — but, as a group, they still tend to spend shorter periods on benefit than divorced mothers, or indeed than widowed mothers. The lowest figure for more than 5 years duration is for separated wives, at 12.4 per cent, but many of these may simply transfer to another category on divorce.

Children Without Fathers

Murray is not only concerned about 'welfare dependency'. His central argument on single mothers is based on the undesirable effects on the children and on the community of the absence of fathers. The child of a single mother is 'without a father from day one' (he says) and the ensuing discussion implies that this child spends his or her whole childhood without a father. But the principal reason that single mothers do not spend long years as lone mothers on benefit is that they marry — and introduce a father into the household by so doing.

Ermisch has shown that single mothers end their lone parenthood through marriage faster than other lone parents.[1] Their median duration as single lone parents is 35 months, compared with 59 months for women who become lone parent through marriage breakdown. By the time the child is 5 years old, 60 per cent of single mothers have married, and 70 per cent by the time the child is 7 years.

---

[1] John Ermisch, *The Economics of the Family: Applications to Divorce and Re-marriage*, Discussion Paper No. 40, CEPR, London, 1986.

CHESTER COLLEGE LIBRARY

46

Ermisch's study was based on a large 1980 survey, and in 1990 may have to be modified. But the change is less likely to be a longer duration of fatherlessness, than an increase in cohabitation rather than marriage. It is a change that may also be reducing remarriage rates after divorce and widowhood. Among women aged 18-49, with and without children, the proportion cohabiting has risen from 9 per cent of single women and 39 per cent of divorced and separated women 1981, to 20 per cent of single and 52 per cent of divorced and separated women in 1988.[1]

Given these patterns, pointing the finger at single mothers — but not at divorced or separated wives — as an especial danger to society makes little sense. If, for a child, being brought up without a father is of key importance, it is hard to see a difference of major social significance between starting life without a father and then acquiring one, and starting life with a father and then losing him, even though it might have been better for the child in both cases if there had been a stable union involving both natural parents.

Neighbourhoods of Lone Mothers

Moreover, Murray's picture of whole neighbourhoods dominated by lone mothers has to be looked at twice. It is undesirable that housing policies, both national and local, have resulted in the undue concentration of one-parent families in poor neighbourhoods, often in the least desirable property. But this says more about our treatment of one-parent families than about the 'contaminating' influence of single mothers. In any case, the one-parent families in the area cannot all be single mothers. And since many lone mothers will marry or in the case of divorced and widowed mothers, remarry, they cannot be judged to be offering an example of a permanent rejection of marriage or of the role of men in families.

---

[1] 'General Household Survey: Preliminary Results for 1988', *OPCS Monitor*, 5 December 1989.

Murray's thesis may have been exaggerated for effect, so as to get his main point over, but making scapegoats of single mothers for society's ills does not help us to approach the serious issues raised by the growing proportion of one-parent families. This growth has to be seen in the context of changes in social attitudes across the wider society. We live in an age when (according to the British Social Attitudes Survey for 1983) over 90 per cent of those aged between 18 and 34 do not consider pre-marital sex to be particularly wrong, and when divorce and cohabitation are increasing and are being seen as acceptable at all levels of society. We may want to seek ways to counter these developments at an individual level, but is not easy to see how we can turn back the clock to a less permissive age — short of a massive religious revival or draconian laws which attempt to control private behaviour between adults.

'Back to the Past'

Nor is it easy to see the practicality of the 'back to the past' solution of social reorganisation based on local community empowerment. Even if a local community could exercise any substantial control over its own affairs in a free market economy, where decisions taken outside the community and sometimes thousands of miles away can destroy its economic base — and at times its social base also — and within a housing market in which housing mobility is reserved for those with ample resources, there would have to be doubts about such a solution to the issues raised by one-parent families. Local control may have advantages in many spheres, but past experience suggests that it also involves harsh and unjust decisions to punish and exclude those judged — by those exercising local influence and power — as undesirable.

The solution Murray does not recommend — though he obviously hankers after — is to make severe cuts in benefits for lone mothers. But, for my part, I have never seen the social morality of storming the barricades over the bodies of living children. The reform of our society ought not to require the sacrifice of the 1.6 million children currently in one-parent families.

Reducing Welfare Dependence

The reality is that, practically and ethically, we have to start from where we are. That means we have to be prepared to put effort and resources into programmes aimed at strengthening the two-parent family — if only because the breakdown of relationships, whether before or during marriage creates so much unhappiness for parents and children. But we must also seek to strengthen the ability of one-parent families to offer their children a sound family life, for as long as they hold that status. And we need policies which neither discourage marriage or remarriage, nor put on economic pressure to enter new unions which have an obvious risk of failure, given the increasing level of second divorces involving children.

If we want to reduce welfare dependence, and ensure that lone mothers are not isolated from society and from general community life and values, then we have to tackle the obstacles that prevent lone mothers from combining home responsibilities and the interests of the children with paid employment. And we have to deal with another major problem — not mentioned by Murray — the large scale failure of absent fathers to meet their responsibilities for the support of their children. That means facing up to the need for a substantial reform of the maintenance system.

Finally, it ought to be said that Murray is right to argue that all the social trends he described began before 1979. But he is wrong to exonerate a Government which has been in power for over ten years, claims to be the party of the family, but has signally failed to address the need for a coherent and properly resourced family policy.

4

BLAMING THE VICTIMS

Alan Walker

In virtually every decade this century a concerted attempt has been made in Britain to separate two groups of poor people: those whose poverty is caused by factors largely beyond their control and those whose behaviour contributes in large measure to their own poverty. The proposition that this latter group poses a threat to the social order often lurks somewhere in this sort of analysis (and, as Nicholas Deakin points out, this apocalyptic variation on the underclass thesis has been advanced by both extremes of the political spectrum). In the dying weeks of the last decade Charles Murray made a serious bid for the role of social policy Cassandra of the 1980s, a role that he had already secured in the US.

In fact, as Murray suggests, the distinction between deserving and undeserving poor goes back much further, at least 500 years in this country. It is particularly favoured by the political Right because it panders to their underlying belief in individual responsibility and minimum intervention by the state in welfare. Thus it was no surprise at all to find Murray, one of the champions of the 1980s neo-liberal thinking on social policy in the US, staking his claim. What was surprising, perhaps, was that he did so with such conviction in a country where, in his own words, he is ignorant of 'all sorts of special conditions'. Despite this the conclusion he reaches is unequivocal: Britain has an underclass and it is growing rapidly.

There are two main deficiencies to Murray's thesis. In the first place he fails to provide any scientific proof that an underclass exists. Substituting for such evidence are innuendos, assertions

50

and anecdotes. Secondly, as a guide to policy, his thesis is, at best, misleading and, at worst, a dangerous diversion from the major problems of poverty and deprivation facing Britain.

In Search of the Underclass

The essence of Murray's argument is that an underclass consists of not necessarily the poorest people, but those of a different type who behave differently not just from the middle class but, crucially, from other poor people as well. They define themselves as different, in Murray's terms, by their parenting, criminal and labour market behaviour, though there is no scientific justification for the selection of these particular criteria nor for the change in behaviour that is supposed to take place when benefits rise above a certain 'threshold'. Thus, stripped to its bare essentials, it is the poor that are to blame for their poverty because they choose to act in certain deviant ways or are conditioned to do so.

In social policy and practical terms, the belief that some poor people are poor because they do not conform to prevailing social values and therefore need to be disciplined may be traced from the repression of vagrancy under the Elizabethan Poor Law, to the workhouse test of the 1834 Poor Law Amendment Act, to the 1930s genuinely-seeking-work test, to the voluntary unemployment rules, YTS and Restart programmes of the 1980s.

A similar legacy may be traced, in intellectual and research terms, from the beginning of this century. Early theories concerning social pathology were heavily influenced by eugenicists, with both official and independent studies being conducted into the inheritance of physical and mental defects. With characteristic foresight Barbara Wootton's critique of this research tradition provided a rebuttal of Murray's piece exactly 30 years before he wrote it.[1] For instance there is his methodological failure to test the permanence or otherwise of underclass status and, especially, his failure to distinguish between the impact of personal inad-

---

[1] Barbara Wootton, *Social Science and Social Pathology*, London: Allen & Unwin, 1959.

equacy and simple economic misfortune. In the late 1950s
attention turned from biological to cultural transmission. First, in
the USA, researchers such as Oscar Lewis examined lower-class
slum settlements in cities like San Juan and concluded that there
was a culture of poverty distinct from poverty. Lewis' work has
been the subject of conclusive scientific criticisms — including its
lack of representativeness, the absence of specification or
quantification of the sub-culture, internal contradictions and the
impossibility of testing the thesis — several of which may be
applied with equal force to Murray's analysis. Britain's variation
on the culture of poverty thesis was the 'cycle of deprivation'
first put forward by none other than Sir Keith Joseph, in a pre-
Thatcherite guise, back in 1972. The central idea was that
poverty persists because social problems reproduce themselves
from one generation to the next and, specifically, that inadequate
parents tend to rear inadequate children.

Mr Murray's thesis fits very neatly into this ideological and
theoretical legacy, with its characteristic mixture of popular
stereotypes, prejudice about the causes of poverty and ill-founded
quasi-scientific notions. It is indicative that the language Murray
uses to describe the underclass echoes the medical models of the
past: 'disease', 'plague', 'contamination'. However, it is with the
bold statement 'the underclass does not refer to degree of
poverty, but to a type of poverty' that he squarely identifies
himself with this approach. Thus he not only separates a type of
poor person from others but also personalises the causes of this
type of poverty, with a strong whiff of the public accusations of
fault and attribution of stigma associated with past eras. His
explanation of underclass poverty represents a blend of both
cultural and cycle of deprivation elements, including parenting
behaviour and contamination by association.

Is There an Underclass?

This approach to poverty, of which Charles Murray's rather
idiosyncratic notion of an underclass is but the latest variation,
has already been demolished by the overwhelming weight of

scientific evidence against it. For example, didn't anyone tell Mr Murray that Sir Keith Joseph prompted a massive research programme in the 1970s devoted to his then pet theory: nearly £1 million, 37 different studies producing 20 books and a mountain of papers. One of the main findings of this programme was that there is no simple continuity of social problems between generations of the sort implied then by Joseph and now by Murray.

> At least half of the children born into a disadvantaged home do not repeat the pattern of disadvantage in the next generation. Over half of all forms of disadvantage arise anew each generation.[1]

Or, as the final report on this programme put it, 'continuities are by no means inevitable and there is no general sense in which "like begets like"'.[2] As Murray knows, very similar findings emerged from the research on the American War on Poverty in the late 1960s.

What this research and a vast amount of subsequent scientific work shows is *not* that poor people are alienated from society, have different values or behave differently (when we allow for the devastating impact that poverty has on behaviour) but, rather, their remarkable assimilation into the attitudes, values and aspirations of British society. There is plenty of contemporary research evidence. Murray singles out a supposed difference between younger and older people in attitudes towards employment as one of the three legs of his case. But, contrary to his anecdotes, a recent representative study of young long-term unemployed men and women found that they placed very great importance on having jobs.

> This was demonstrated by their continued search for employment in the face of repeated failure and disappointment, and in their

---

[1] Rutter, M. and Madge, N., *Cycles of Disadvantage*, London: Heinemann, 1976, p. 304.
[2] Brown, M. and Madge, N., *Despite the Welfare State*, London: Heinemann, 1982, p. 143.

> willingness to stay in jobs which were poorly-paid or otherwise unattractive just to avoid further unemployment... In interview after interview, the advice these young people offered themselves, and others like them, was to *keep looking, don't give up.*[1]

Murray's data on economic activity are from 1981, the height of the last recession in Britain when school-leavers faced unemployment rates of up to 50 per cent. (The recession itself and the surge of unemployment that resulted from it was, in large part, the result of the government's own policies.) Research among the 'aristocracy' of skilled labour in Sheffield during this period, the fathers of the young people Murray criticises, showed how even their commitment to employment was ground down by the sheer hopelessness of their search for work.[2] Is it any surprise that, during this period, young people quickly learnt the reality of the labour market from their fathers before they themselves faced it? Furthermore, the fact that some young people reject YTS places is not sufficient to attribute deviant status to them — many such schemes *are* slave labour and the programme has a notoriously poor safety record (a fatal accident rate of 138.2 per 100,000 trainees) — unless, that is, membership of the underclass is determined solely on the basis of Mr Murray's or Mrs Thatcher's values.

As far as the main element of his case is concerned — the growth of illegitimacy — the evidence similarly offers him little comfort. (As it happens the legal concept of illegitimacy was abolished by the Family Law Reform Act, 1987.) The latest official figures show that at least half of the children born outside marriage in 1986, in fact, had parents who were living together.[3] In other words, the union may not have been sanctified by marriage but the children were living within a stable family, with a father. This simply demonstrates, among other things, that

[1] McRae, S., *Young and Jobless*, London: PSI, 1987, p. 144.
[2] Westergaard, J., Noble, I. and Walker, A., *After Redundancy*, Oxford: Polity Press, 1989.
[3] CSO, *Social Trends 1989*, London: HMSO, 1989, p. 47.

54

attitudes towards marriage are changing. This conclusion is backed-up by figures on conceptions among people under the age of 20. While the proportion of such births inside marriage halved between 1975 and 1985, the proportion outside marriage but jointly registered rose by three times. Some three out of five illegitimate births to women under 20 are jointly registered.

This is not to suggest that illegitimacy should not be regarded as a social issue but rather that Mr Murray has got it a little out of proportion. The illegitimacy rate in Denmark is more than double Britain's and, as far as I know, that society is not on the brink of disaster. Moreover, in Britain the data show that marriage breakdown is the main cause of lone parenthood, not illegitimacy.

In the end it is not clear whether it is illegitimacy, as he says, or lone parenthood that worries Murray. Whichever it is, the prospect he conjures up of a plague of young single mothers contaminating whole neighbourhoods is, quite simply, ridiculous. As Joan Brown showed in her recent study of lone parents on benefit, Murray's image of young single mothers represents only a small minority of lone parents.

> If there is a typical lone parent, it is a separated or divorced woman. The children involved may be very young, but are more likely to be over 5 years...[1]

Murray does not mention the duration of lone parenthood status — surely a key variable for his underclass thesis? British research indicates that single, never-married women leave lone parenthood more quickly than divorced women: their median duration as lone parents is 35 months compared with 59 months for women who become lone parents as a result of marriage breakdown.[2]

---

[1] Joan Brown, *Why Don't They Go to Work? Mothers on Benefit*, London: HMSO, 1989, p. 10.

[2] John Ermisch, *The Economics of the Family: Applications to Divorce and Re-marriage*, London: CEPR, 1986.

If this sort of evidence is not sufficient to convince Mr Murray that he is barking up the wrong tree he need look no further than the case studies published alongside his article in *The Sunday Times Magazine*.[1] Purporting to be examples of life among the underclass in North Peckham what they actually illustrate are attitudes and values, for example, towards bringing-up children, that are more in tune with the rest of society than at odds with it.

So, there is no evidence of a separate type of poverty, still less of a sub-culture or sub-strata alienated from the rest of society and with different values from it, or of a process of transmission or contamination.

The Growing Divide

Let me be clear, I am not arguing that there is no problem and we have nothing to worry about. It is just that the research evidence compels me to see the issue completely differently from Mr Murray: the problem concerns the degree of poverty and not the type of poverty.

The problem of poverty, significant in the 1970s, has worsened substantially in the 1980s. At the same time, uniquely in post-war Britain, the slight trend towards a narrowing of differentials in income and wealth has been thrown into reverse. This has been a conscious act of Government policy, comprising, briefly, cuts in benefits for the poorest and cuts in taxation for the richest.[2] This has created a rapid and massive polarisation of living standards. At one extreme there is a severely deprived group whose behaviour is predictably influenced by their abject poverty but who still do not resemble an underclass in any sociological sense. The only reason they, in Murray's words, 'live in a different world' is that they have no choice. Some, for

[1] 26 November, 1989.
[2] Walker, A. and Walker, C., (eds.), *The Growing Divide*, London: CPAG, 1987.

56

example, are lone parents who have been clustered together as an act of housing management.

At the other extreme are a growing number of very wealthy people (an 'overclass' Mr Murray?). As an act of social policy gross inequalities, unknown in Britain for at least 100 years, have been created. This polarisation brings with it segregation. Witness the building of security fences around some of the new private or privatised housing developments in London's docklands, so that the rich can live in a different world from the poor. This new segregation is being exacerbated by Government policies towards public welfare services, such as health and education, which have been cut back while the private sector has been subsidised; a policy designed to produce private affluence and public squalor.

These two extremes have been openly engineered by Government policy, and the massive inequalities underlying them are two parts of the same problem. To paraphrase Tawney, what thoughtful rich people may refer to as the problem of poverty thoughtful poor people may call the problem of wealth. Only the rose-tinted spectacles of neo-liberal ideological commitment could fail to see the adverse transformation that British society has undergone in the last decade of Thatcherism. The idea that the Government's social policies do not depart from those of previous governments is a crude attempt to avoid the compelling facts. Read the evidence, Mr Murray. For example, the Family Policy Studies Centre has just shown how Government income support policies are adversely affecting families and creating destitution among 16-18 year olds.[1] The latest report from the National Association of Citizens Advice Bureaux catalogues the hardship and high levels of unmet need as poor families are refused money to buy the most basic and essential everyday items.[2] These are but recent examples of an overwhelming indictment of the Government's policies.

[1] Roll, J., *Young People: Growing Up in The Welfare State*, London: FPSC, 1990.
[2] *Hard Times for Social Fund Applicants*, London: NACAB, 1990.

The Poverty of Mr Murray's Policies

This brings me to the other major defect of Murray's analysis: his policy conclusions. The cause of the problem is 'well meaning' (*sic*) government intervention; the answer is to remove the influence of government. This Alexandrian solution was set out at length in his book *Losing Ground*[1] but then, as now, there was no evidence that this would either help or at least not make things worse. It is, after all, incumbent on Murray to demonstrate that his radical solution would not repeat the horrors of earlier and contemporary free markets. The tyranny of the welfare state, as he sees it, could well be replaced by a far fiercer tyranny of various unfettered corporate or neighbourhood welfare states.

So what should be done? A policy to combat poverty and the increasing social polarisation of British society would include a significant redistribution of income from rich to poor, reversing the £50,000 million cut from the income tax of the top 10 per cent of wage earners since 1979 which has caused some of the problem; the 'universal' targeting of social security for example on families, through child benefit, and people with disabilities, through a comprehensive disability income scheme; and a minimum wage to ensure that the 'deserving' poor (who Murray strangely excluded from his account) are not exploited. A longer-term strategy would seek to ensure that all of the nation's resources are geared more effectively to meeting need.[2] In addition measures must be taken to liberate poor people and other service (public and private) users from bureaucracy and excessive restrictions on their self-determination. Here our analyses touch fleetingly. However, I would pursue this empowerment through legal citizenship rights to welfare and employment which would, of course, be coupled with duties such as paid employment, caring and other forms of social reproduction.

---

[1] New York: Basic Books, 1984.

[2] The Sheffield Group, *The Social Economic and the Democratic State*, London: Lawrence and Wishart, 1989.

58

Murray's Thesis is Misleading

Herein lies what is probably the most important shortcoming of
Murray's thesis: it is misleading, perhaps wilfully so. It diverts
attention, on the one hand, from the real problems: pauperiz-
ation and social segregation as acts of Government policy. On
the other hand, it misleads policy-makers and the general public
into believing that poverty is a residual personal, family or
neighbourhood issue, rather than a widespread one. This is a
serious matter because arguments such as Murray's diminish the
scale and complexity of the problem facing society in combating
poverty, and encourage the belief that comparatively simple and
inexpensive policies can be effective. Because it minimises the
problem it is likely to be superficially attractive to people outside
of Murray's ideological rut: it allows poverty to be acknowledged
but does not imply that we should feel guilty about it. In other
words, Mr Murray's underclass, like all previous attempts to
individualise the causes of poverty, diverts our attention from
blaming the mechanisms through which resources are distributed,
including the role of the Government, to blaming, in William
Ryan's famous phrase, 'the victims'.

5

MR MURRAY'S ARK

Nicholas Deakin

For the second time in twenty years, the British social science community has received a peremptory summons to accept that an imminent crisis of the underclass is upon us. At the end of the 1960s, it was younger Marxist critics who perceived inevitable conflict arising from the frustrated aspirations of an exploited sub-proletariat largely composed of immigrant workers; now it is Conservatives who warn us — in equally doomladen terms — of inevitable contamination of the values and standards of our society through the growth of a culturally distinct and undeserving urban lumpenproletariat. On each occasion, we have been told, our complacency has blinded us both to the true facts and the wrath to come.

Murray's Tripod

Well, as Mr Murray himself might put it, maybe so. But on this occasion, as on the last, the evidence that is being deployed strikes me as a mite less than wholly compelling. Murray's case for the existence of his version of the underclass phenomenon rests on a tripod — increases in numbers of 'illegitimate' births, rising crime rates and growth in unemployment — two legs of which are distinctly shaky. Take illegitimacy. This (in Murray's conception) represents 'the purest form of being without parents' and as such constitutes one of the sharpest hazards to the development of normal community life: it removes the male parent from the key role he should play in the developmental process through which responsible future citizens must pass. The difficulty with this concept — which Murray himself has to concede — is that half those born 'illegitimate' have their two parents living together at the time of birth; and that many of these relationships will in due course result in the marriage of the natural parents. Alternatively, their mother may either marry or cohabit with another man, thereby providing a surrogate male parent for her children. Why step-parents do not feature in Murray's account is a mystery, given the exceptionally rapid growth over the last decade of families that are thus 'reconstituted' (in demographers' argot).

Generally, the point cannot be too strongly stressed that single parenthood — regarded by many Conservatives as a form of moral plague ('the most socially subversive institution of our time' according to P. Johnson) — is not a static condition, still less an immoral one. Rather, it is a stage in the life cycle which may lead in a variety of different directions, with widely various consequences. The decline in the popularity of marriage, which has helped to produce higher rates of 'illegitimacy' is itself a stage in a process of development which is taking this country in the direction not of the American model (which, as Murray rightly points out, is far more heavily influenced by the race factor than our own) but the Scandinavian. Sweden and Denmark already have illegitimacy rates twice as high as those in this country; yet the great majority of children there are born into two-parent families and civil society has survived without the dire consequences with which Murray threatens us.

Crime Rates

Crime rates, Murray's second exhibit, need not detain us long. No-one who (like the present writer) has had first-hand acquaintance with the collection of criminal statistics would dream of using them as the basis for a theory of social change. But, since Murray is quite properly interested as much in perceptions of the prevalence of violent crime as in its actual incidence, it is odd that he did not think fit to consult the British Crime Survey. The contrasts that this shows between popular anxieties and realities could perhaps be said to 'force theory to its knees', in Murray's colourful phrase — unhappily, his is the theory that ends in that uncomfortable posture.

Unemployment

On unemployment, Murray is on much firmer ground. Paradoxically, data disappear abruptly from sight at this stage in his argument — presumably because the Government's tampering with the unemployment statistics has made comparison over time virtually impossible. Despite these misconceived attempts to hold up the weather by breaking the bloody glass, however, it seems clear that the rapid growth in unemployment which began at the end of the 1970s (not 'late' in the 1970s, incidentally, when it was going down: Mr Murray is Tebbiting here) has been the single most significant factor in increasing poverty during the 1980s. It has also had a differential impact, by class, region, age, and race. Murray is absolutely right to insist on the central importance of this factor and on its potentially long lasting consequences, in terms of the experience of a whole generation of young people who were unable to obtain entry to the labour market. What he could have added — but didn't — is that much of this growth in unemployment can be directly attributed to the Government's own policies (half, at least, according to an authoritative analysis by the House of Lords Select Committee on Unemployment (1983)).

Consideration of where to go next makes up the remainder of Murray's contribution, which is mostly remarkable for its scepticism about the role of governments, present and future. In fact, given that the mass unemployment of the 1980s was fuelled by Government policies, it is logical enough to suppose that changing them (both policies and Government) is a more promising way of starting to achieve lasting reductions than statistical juggling. Since the Government currently seems determined to repeat the mistakes of the early 1980s and squeeze British industry once again within an inch of its life or beyond, with a concomitant repetition of the disastrous pattern of job losses — but this time in services as well as manufacturing — this task is rapidly becoming urgent.

Benefits

The issue of benefits is more complex. Mr Murray is to be commended for refusing to buy the nostrum being peddled by the British New Right moralists. He has no objection to providing basic support for single parents and their children through the early stages of child rearing; but persists in seeing an element of perverse incentives in providing generously beyond that point. Evidently, the cultural arguments weigh more strongly with him than the public health ones (having praised Frank Field's recent work on the underclass, Murray should now reread Field on the persistence of class differentials in mortality). Here, child benefit is vital in helping to float single parents successfully through the dependent stage when their children are young to the point when they can re-enter the labour market. Some of them already do — 45 per cent of mothers with children aged 3-4, for example — despite 'overwhelming constraints in terms of lack of job opportunities, the availability of only low-paid work and the difficulties of providing child care'.[1] Forms of assistance that would enable them to do so in larger numbers are a crucial policy priority. Labour market policies as well as benefits need to be adjusted (compare with the successful Swedish model); more support from Government, in the form of cash as well as improved quality and availability of child care services, is a legitimate national investment — as Eleanor Rathbone pointed out long before Beveridge.

'Little Platoons'

Perhaps the most interesting passage in Mr Murray's otherwise sparse list for action is the one he hardly develops at all; the

---

[1] Janet Lewis, 'Lone Parent Families', *Journal of Social Policy*, October 1989.

notion that much of the work on breaking up (or down) the underclass (if it does indeed exist) will have to be done at the local level. Here, the centripetal tendencies of Thatcher Government policies have inflicted quite unnecessary damage on the capacity of localities to take effective initiatives. Murray calls for 'a massive dose of self-government'; fine, but where are the resources, human and financial to come from? He airily asserts that it is easy to combine sustaining current levels of expenditure for public systems with decentralised control over them. I do not think he can have much recent acquaintance with HM Treasury, and its present attitudes towards public expenditure.

Here again, it is reversal of existing policy that supplies the logical starting point; the experiments in decentralisation of service delivery and local control which began under the banner of 'municipal socialism' in the 1980s, whose success was compromised by the Government's vendetta against local authorities, need to be re-examined and the lessons applied (and if Mr Murray believes that such measures have not yet been seriously explored he should forthwith consult the oracles — at Bristol, for example).

Elsewhere, (in *In Pursuit*[1]), Mr Murray has argued, if I have understood him correctly, for a systematic devolution of power to the 'little platoons' (one more time, that old Burkean rag). These are to be essentially voluntary associations acting independently of the state. Withdrawal by the state from service delivery will allow the individual citizen to earn his civic status by showing that he is 'pulling his own weight'. Those who do not, like single-parent families, will need 'prodding' into recognition of the need to do so. Alternatively, they should find refuge among their own kind, and allow neighbourhoods which value two-parent status to flourish without contamination.

---

[1] New York: Simon & Schuster, 1988.

64

Concealed Authoritarianism

To which I would respond: neighbourhood autonomy by all means; but not through the imposition of artificial homogeneity of values, class composition, or even race. One key difficulty with the platoon as an image is its barely concealed authoritarianism: with Burke as our patron saint, distinctions of rank and degree cannot fail to be faithfully observed. If they are not, how are essential services to be supplied to the autonomous neighbourhood: the 'innumerable servile, degrading, unseemly, unmanly, and often most unwholesome and pestiferous occupations to which by the social economy so many wretches are inevitably doomed' (Burke again)? No doubt these wretches can be bussed in from outside; but isn't that a trifle, well, South African?

Nor am I clear how far Murray would allow welfare policy to be a matter of local discretion. It is not difficult to imagine local control that leads straight back to the Poor Law — Elizabethan, that is, which had a particularly vigorous line in prodding those whose occupations or morals did not square with local values.

Democracy

The virtues of some form of local control are not in doubt: any dispute is about how it is to be exercised — who is accountable to whom for which activities. There is an implicit pessimism (cynicism, even) about the form that Murray advocates and the limits he sets, as when he comments — ironically, I assume — that poverty 'needn't bother us as long as it stays in its own part of town'. At root, this pessimism springs from scepticism about democracy and the possibility of articulating choices through disinterested debate within a democratic system. In their pessimism, Marxist and Conservative once again join hands. To them, democracy merely provides the screen behind which the executive committee of the bourgeoisie or the self-aggrandizement of the bureau maximiser can function unchallenged. Personally, I find it dispiriting that an American, of all people, should be preaching the virtues of a static form of society composed of neatly docketed and differentiated small units from which the dangerous classes have been carefully excluded.

But perhaps we can take some comfort from Mr Murray's recognition that 'Britain in 1989 has resources that make predicting the course of the underclass on the basis of the US experience very dicey'. As in the late 1960s, the clouds may roll over without shedding their rain. Even if some drops do fall, it may be best not to rush to embark in Mr Murray's Ark quite yet — at least, until we know how soundly constructed it really is.

6

REJOINDER

Charles Murray

Introduction

I picked up the four responses to *Underclass* gloomily, having been through this sort of thing before and not looking forward to doing it again. But, as I read, I became progressively more cheerful, finally laughing out loud when Nicholas Deakin parenthetically admonished me for 'Tebbiting' because I argued that British unemployment had grown in the 'late' 1970s rather than at the 'end'. In the US, where this sort of thrust and parry is generally conducted with maces, no-one could have raised a quibble — but a well-taken quibble — so gracefully and good-naturedly. In any case, let me begin by saying that I thought the papers by Field, Brown, and Deakin, do not really require a rejoinder for the best of reasons: their commentaries fairly and resourcefully defend a point of view that I attacked; I am, nevertheless, unpersuaded, for reasons that I think were already stated adequately in my original article; and I will be satisfied if the reader simply goes back and takes another look at *Underclass* side-by-side with their observations. My own comments about these commentaries are less in the form of rebuttal than an attempt to minimise confusion and maximise authentic disagreement.

I should add that I enjoyed Professor Walker's paper as well, albeit in another way. It is the kind of undiluted statement of Left dogma on this topic that is fast disappearing — a sort of modern Rousseauism in which the noble savage is replaced by the noble poor person — written, as the rules apparently require, so as to convey that the Left's intellectual adversaries are not only wrong, but incompetent; not only incompetent, but sinister. And so to the main points at issue.

Is there a legitimate behavioural distinction to be drawn among classes of poor people?

If I had to pick out the one point on which confusion is most intertwined with real disagreement, it would be the question of whether an underclass exists at all. Even when the word is admitted, people use it differently. Frank Field's usage is quite different from mine, for example, defining the underclass by condition (the very frail elderly pensioner, the long-term unemployed, and the poor single parent), whereas I defined it by behaviour — some long-term unemployed are members of the underclass, others, like the long-term unemployed family in Birkenhead that I cited in *Underclass*, are unequivocally not. Some single mothers qualify; others do not, and so forth. I would exclude frail, elderly pensioners altogether — the problem represented by the frail, elderly pensioner with too little money is that he has too little money, and the problem is solved (more or less) by giving him more money. Questions of moral hazard arise only at second or third hand. Questions of present behaviour arise not at all.

When I use the term 'underclass' I am indeed focusing on a certain type of poor person defined not by his condition, e.g. long-term unemployed, but by his deplorable behaviour in response to that condition, e.g. unwilling to take the jobs that are available to him. The question remains, however, whether there is an empirical reality behind my statements about deplorable behaviour. Walker thinks not, emphatically. Science has conducted surveys, and science has proved that I am deluded — there is, in his words, an 'overwhelming weight of scientific evidence against' the notion of an underclass. And, the nature of this overwhelming weight of evidence? He begins by citing proof that 'At least half of the children born into a disadvantaged home do not repeat the pattern of disadvantage in the next generation'. Then he cited evidence that among a representative sample of young people, many (he did not say what proportion, but presumably it was large) continued to 'search for employment in the face of repeated failure and disappointment'. All of this makes sense to me. In fact, I am a little surprised that the proportion who 'repeat the pattern of disadvantage' is as high as 50 per cent. As for unemployment, I am already on record in *Underclass*, when I wrote that 'I am not suggesting that a third or a quarter or even a fifth of lower-class young people are indifferent to work', for example.

This points to a larger misreading of *Underclass* which, though common among my critics, remains mystifying to me. How can people read my extensive descriptions of causation, all of which focus on the ways in which members are responding sensibly (at least in the short term) to policies that have been put in place around them, and then cite surveys regarding a 'culture of poverty' to refute me? The burden of my argument is that members of the underclass are *not* sunk in a cultural bog; that all people who are poor do *not* repeat the cycle of disadvantage, whereas others do, and the interesting question is why the latter group (which has existed from time immemorial) has existed in such different proportions in different societies at different times, and in the industrialised west seems, in recent years, to have grown rapidly. I am arguing for disaggregation of the data about poor people. Which segments of the poor population 'repeat the pattern of disadvantage'? Are they randomly scattered throughout people below a certain income level, or are there common elements among them? Which segments of the unemployed search diligently for work and which do not? I am arguing that there is an ecology to poverty. Cross-sectional surveys of poor people or of the unemployed that detail population parameters are useless in either confirming or disconfirming this hypothesis.

70

Observational Evidence

If one wants to talk about evidence on this topic, the richest and most informative evidence is in the form of observation, and the library is large. Let me make a statement as sweeping as Walker's about overwhelming evidence: regarding the United States, I know of no scientific observational study of poor communities in America, beginning with W.E.B. DuBois' pioneering *The Philadelphia Negro* in 1890 that does *not* describe class difference within low-income populations that conform to my distinction between poor people and the underclass. There is interesting distinction here worth pondering: those who say that there is no underclass tend to rely on studies in which scholars go into poor neighbourhoods for a few hours at a time with clipboards and multiple-choice questionnaires. Those who say there is an underclass tend to rely on studies in which scholars live in poor communities, and get their information from long conversations conducted over weeks and months with the people who live there.

Because I am not nearly as familiar with the literature in Britain, I will content myself with this additional sweeping observation, and readers may judge from their own experience whether it is true: The people who deal most intimately with poor communities in their daily lives use the same distinction among poor people that I use. The managers of council estates, policemen in poor neighbourhoods, social workers, nurses, and physicians, may or may not bridle at the term 'underclass', but if the topic of conversation is not whether this American reactionary is right, but rather a leisurely discussion of how these people go about their work and what life is like in the communities where they work, the distinction between the good folks and the underclass shines through after the first five minutes.

However we need not continue this debate endlessly. Regarding unemployment at least, there is a simple, fairly conclusive test that I suggested in *Underclass* and hereby propose once more. Find a philanthropist or government agency that will fund a few hundred full-time, low-skill jobs at decent pay. Get to a poor urban neighbourhood convenient to the job site. Seek out a representative sample of unemployed young men, and ask each if he wants a job. Almost all will say yes, probably accompanied by many harsh words about Mrs Thatcher. Then offer them the jobs you have available. Record their behavioural response to this opportunity. Count who does what. Follow those who actually take the jobs for the next year. And you will have your answer, or much of the answer, to the size and nature of the underclass among unemployed young men.

What is the comparative role of individual behaviour and structural causes?

Am I blaming the victim, as Walker insists? In one sense, obviously not. I am blaming governments for wrong-headed policies that seduce people into behaving in ways that seem sensible in the short term but are disastrous in the long term.

In a second sense, blame does not come into the argument at all. I am simply observing that a behaviour exists and that it has pernicious social consequences. If my critics were to prove to me irrefutably that the people who are behaving in these deplorable ways are in no way free agents, it would not change anything in my analysis.

In a third sense, I am using the concept of blame as a useful fiction. America's Jesse Jackson puts it well when he tells black teenagers that 'It may not be your fault if someone knocks you down, but it's your fault if you don't get up'. I put it somewhat differently in *Losing Ground* when I wrote that even if it is true that a poor young person is not responsible for the condition in which he finds himself, the worst thing one can do is try to persuade him of that.

The Importance of Blame

In a fourth sense, I want to reintroduce the notion of blame, and sharply reduce our readiness to call people 'victims', for this compelling reason: British intellectuals and (despite Mrs Thatcher) British social policy remain overwhelmingly on the side

of the poor youngster who fails in school, gets in trouble with
the law, does not hold a job, or has a child without being able
to care for it. Youths who do any of these things will find no
shortage of social workers and academics prepared to make
excuses to try to shield them from the consequences of their
behaviour. I am more concerned about the poor youngster who
is studying hard, obeying the law, working hard, and taking care
not to have a baby. Forget (for a moment) about the ethics and
just deserts of this situation and consider hard-headedly that
Britain badly needs lots of young people to behave in these
desirable ways, and the straightforward way to achieve that end
is in a context where such behaviour is praised and rewarded.
The difficulty is that, by taking away responsibility — by saying,
'Because the system is to blame, it's not your fault that...' —
society also takes away the credit that is an essential part of the
reward structure that fosters social and economic mobility. It is
impossible to tell someone persuasively that he did well regarding
one form of behaviour unless he may also be told that he did
badly regarding another. Blame is essential if one is to praise.

Moral Judgement

In a fifth sense — yes, Professor Walker, your deepest fears are
justified — I do want to reintroduce the notion of genuine blame
in a moral sense. The standard to which I hold myself, and which
I advocate for other commentators on social policy, is: do not
apply a different moral standard to strangers — including poor
strangers — from the standard which applies to the people one
knows and loves. I bring moral judgement to bear on the
behaviour of my children, wife, friends — and myself. If I say of
strangers that they are exempt, why? Because they are less
intelligent? My own childhood environment left something to be
desired. So did the environment that my children grew up in.
The environment that my parents grew up in was plain awful.
We are all indeed brothers and sisters under the skin, and we
deserve the respect of being held accountable.

To bring moral judgement to bear does not mean Cromwellian severity. If one of my daughters, single and without the resources to raise a child on her own, comes home pregnant, I am not obliged to throw her out of the house. But I will think what she did is wrong. Not just a mistake, nor just a miscalculation, but wrong. I will tell her so. I will love her, help her, and think hard thoughts about the male who collaborated, and find fault with myself as a father... but none of that will change the underlying reaction that is in my view essential for the sustenance of a civilized society. I will blame her. If it were somehow possible for government institutions to do the same thing — to love, help, but also to hold people morally responsible for their behaviour — then I would have far fewer objections to social programmes, for I think they would do far more good and far less harm. Unfortunately, we do not know how to make governmental institutions act that way.

Is illegitimacy really such a terrible problem?

Joan Brown's handling of the data regarding lone births, marriages, and cohabitation, adds significantly to my description in *Underclass*; and the contrasts between the British and American situation are well-taken. Regarding Britain, however, I am not sure, that the data she cites portray a picture much different from the one I portrayed.

The case she makes, with general agreement from Walker and Deakin, goes roughly like this: yes, births to single women have increased as a proportion of live births, but this does not necessarily mean that the children of these marriages are growing up without fathers. Cohabitation has increased dramatically. Moreover, single women who have babies typically get married within a few years of birth. In contrast to the US experience, only about a quarter of unmarried mothers remain on benefit for as long as five years. Taking these factors together, then, my fears about communities without fathers are overdrawn.

First, a technical addendum to Brown's data: I did not use the Ermisch data that Brown and Walker both cite for a reason to which Brown alludes but which deserves more emphasis: Ermisch's data were based on a representative sample of women aged 16-59 as of 1980, which means that he was examining marital dynamics for women who came to childbearing age beginning in the mid-1930s. The massive change in the proportion of children born to single women began in the late 1970s. This raises two difficulties. The first is a problem of truncation in the data: the youngest women in his sample, whose experience was closest in time to the era in which the illegitimacy problem increased, had 'had time' to experience no more than a few years of lone parenthood before data collection came to an end. If changes in behaviour were occurring regarding remarriage, Ermisch's data could not have revealed it.

The second difficulty is the life experience of a young woman who had a child without a husband in the 1960s and early 1970s is likely to be an uncertain guide in assessing what is going on with such women in the 1980s; the experience of those who had a child without a husband in the 1930s, 1940s and 1950s, is likely to be positively misleading. Nothing in Ermisch's article addresses these potential cohort effects. Perhaps Brown is right in predicting that more recent data will not reveal much change in the average number of years between the birth of a child and eventual marriage (to someone, not necessarily the father). But, based on her own discussion of the number of single mothers who are on benefit for more than five years (probably a good proxy measure for failure to marry), something is happening that suggests changes. It would be illuminating to plot that proportion of long-term recipients from 1970 through 1987 and see what the curve looks like — but I must leave that to Brown, since I do not have that data series presently available to me.

Illegitimacy and Socio-Economic Status

The main point, however, is that the data Brown reviews (even disregarding the technical issues) are consistent with the portrait I drew in *Underclass*. This is most easily seen by trying to translate the statistics on marriage into a playgroup of a dozen children living on a council estate. As I indicated in *Underclass*, illegitimacy in England (as in the US) has a strong inverse statistical association with socio-economic status. Municipalities with large proportions of lower-class households have much higher illegitimacy ratios than municipalities with small proportions of lower-class households; and lower-class neighbourhoods within a given municipality have higher rates than the municipal average. With an overall national ratio of 25 per cent, the typical ratio for a poor municipality is 35-45 per cent, and the ratio within council estates in those communities is by mathematical necessity (given the known socio-economic link) considerably higher.

Applying these considerations to the dozen playmates, what is the likely profile of their family histories and current family situations? Trying to estimate the specific number of children in the various situations would take me far afield — the calculations become statistically quite complex, involving expected values and distributional probabilities for a complicated set of permutations. But even taking the unadorned illegitimacy ratios in poor communities, the numbers Brown cites regarding cohabitation, adding in the additional effects of divorces, and making a rough mental estimate, should make the point plain: only a minority of the dozen children are likely to be living in two-parent families, and almost all will have experienced spells of living in a two-parent family and spells of living with a single parent. Now, add into this picture the flesh and bones of what the parents, the marriages, and the parenting are like.

Here, I think, *Underclass* needed another paragraph elaborating on the experience of one of my informants, the unemployed family in Birkenhead. This exceptionally articulate and thoughtful couple are no fans of Mrs Thatcher's; on the contrary, they are staunch Labourites who hold no brief for my Whig solutions. But the story they told, I cannot stress sufficiently, must be heard by people who are trying to interpret the numbers. Yes, some of the mothers in their neighbourhood around them were cohabiting in a relationship, but this was seldom a plus, more often a negative.

The cohabitations were not those of loving parents, but more often of stormy, highly unstable relationships. In cases where remarriage had occurred, there were few, kindly stepfathers and too many who saw the kids they had inherited as a nuisance. Adding up the women who had never married or cohabited, plus those who were between boyfriends, plus those who were between husbands, plus those who had abusive husbands, and there were very few families.

I will be happy to see the same exercise performed for a playgroup in a middle-class neighbourhood, but readers who are parents will not need to wait for that. All they have to do is think about the playgroup to which their children belong. Yes, there are likely to be some in the group whose parents were divorced. But (I am asserting: do the counting for yourself), the chances are that at any one time a solid majority of the children are living in two-parent households, several of them (probably a majority) are living in households in which there has never been a divorce, and hardly any of the children are living with a mother who has had three, four, or more, live-in partners. Even in a world of high divorce rates in which the breakdown of the family is lamented, the familial world of middle-class and upper-class children is importantly different from the world of the underclass.

Is Cohabitation Equivalent to Marriage?

One final question before leaving this topic, and it is not rhetorical: Why are the British, or at least the British represented among these commentators, so ready to assume that cohabitation means a stable relationship that is more or less equivalent (for purposes of rearing young children) to marriage? I know of nothing in the US experience with cohabitation to suggest confidence. On the contrary, cohabitation often seems as likely to be a minus for the child as a plus. Are there good data on this topic that I do not know about? Or is it just not a done thing in British intellectual circles to think that marriage is fundamentally different from living together?

In this regard, I was struck by the remark by both Walker and Deakin that parts of Scandinavia have illegitimacy rates twice as high as those in Britain and yet 'civil society has survived without the dire consequences with which Murray threatens us' (Deakin) and 'as far as I know, [Denmark] is not on the brink of disaster' (Walker). Reading these comments, I once again had the sense of being in a time warp that stayed with me throughout my conversations with the British while I was researching *Underclass*. As recently as six years ago, when *Losing Ground* was first published, I was constantly responding to praise of Sweden and Denmark, which were held up as models of the welfare state. I almost never hear such statements any more, because the American champions of the Scandinavian model have lately been backpedalling. 'Brink of disaster' is still too strong a term to describe the situation facing Sweden and Denmark, but their problems have been multiplying, and embedded within those problems are ones not nearly as simple as a rise in unemployment, but ones that arise from the difficulties of trying to sustain a society and a culture without the traditional family to rely upon. The jury is still out, but on the dire consequences of illegitimacy rates at 50 per cent, I would offer Messrs. Walker and Deakin a traditional American challenge: want to bet?

Bits and Pieces

Before proceeding to the final large question, two points deserve brief mention: regarding Nicholas Deakin's paragraph about crime, he is too elliptical for me to follow. Does the British Crime Survey that I should have consulted reveal that popular anxieties about crime are greater than the reality warrants? Or is the anxiety less than the reality warrants? In either case, I cannot imagine what he means when he argues that it contradicts anything in my argument. Popular anxieties about crime are wholly irrelevant. My point is that, even after worrying about the problems with the collection of criminal statistics, the changes in violent crime rates in England bespeak a fundamental change in behaviour; that there is reason to think this is not equally a problem in rich communities and poor communities; and that this pertains to the organisation of such communities and the quality of life within them. If Deakin thinks that violent crime has not really risen in England, more or less in the steepening curve that I described, then he should say so. When he says, instead, merely that crime rates 'need not detain us long' and alludes airily to the difficulties of interpreting them, I think that Deakin is perhaps... Tebbiting.

Regarding Frank Field's comment about the distinctive nature of the American underclass, as deriving from the black share-cropper experience in the south: obviously, the British and American situations are different because of the racial experience that blights America's history, and Nick Lemann's work on the relationship of this history to the underclass is provocative and useful. I expected major differences between the underclass in America (mostly black) with the underclass in Britain (mostly white) because of these very different contexts. I was surprised, therefore, to discover how minor the differences were. Life in Birkenhead and Easterhouse was described to me in terms that sounded almost exactly like descriptions of life in South Chicago and East Harlem, the major distinction being that the British underclass is still much less violent than the American underclass. Overall, my experience in Britain tended to reinforce the conclusion that the etiology of the underclass derives more from policy than from cultural context.

What is to be done?

Perhaps the most common reaction to *Underclass* from readers at large is that I neglected or gave too little space to policy recommendations. I did so for a reason that I will state explicitly here.

In my views about policy, I find that I have become (somewhat to my surprise, for I am not temperamentally so) an authentic radical. I am persuaded that a limited central government is not only feasible in the late 20th-century, but would be a far better way to run modern society than the methods we now use. By 'limited central government', I mean a Jeffersonian system in which the central government protects the sanctity of voluntary mutual agreements (including the enforcement of contracts through civil law), and protection of people from physical coercion, and fraud by others (whether they be foreign invaders or the fellow next door). I am not a purist — I think there are other public goods, classically defined, that warrant central government funding and intervention — but I am, by any contemporary understanding, nonetheless, outside the mainstream of politics. Even the more moderate reforms that I am prepared to recommend on grounds that they will make matters better are pretty radical (educational vouchers in place of state education, for example). I do not have in my head that set of policy recommendations that every proper writer about social policy is supposed to have, a list of incremental, politically practicable reforms. I can concoct none that I can persuade myself would do any good.

At the same time, I think my analysis of social problems needs to be considered seriously. Hence the quandary: for me to expand on my policy prescriptions is to give large numbers of readers too easy an excuse for ignoring my analysis of the problem, on grounds that I am obviously a nut. So I do not say much about policy.

But the nature of my views nevertheless creates an abyss separating me from the four commentators on this topic. Professor Walker carries the egalitarian banner without visible second thoughts, leaving me shaking my head that anyone could still be so benighted, just as he doubtless regards me. Joan Brown takes a pragmatic stance, but in doing so presents an underlying dilemma: 'The reality is that, practically and ethically, we have to start from where we are', she writes. 'That means we have to be prepared to put effort and resources into programmes aimed at strengthening the two-parent family... But we must also seek to strengthen the ability of one-parent families to offer their children a sound family life, for as long as they hold that status'.

It cannot be done, in my view. Policies that make the one-parent situation tolerable produce more one-parent families, for the constellation of reasons I discussed in *Underclass*. The strength of the two-parent family is inescapably undermined by those policies. The difficulty in pursuing this line of reasoning, however, is underlined by Brown's remark that 'I have never seen the social morality of storming the barricades over the bodies of living children'. In making social policy, we see the needs and the pains of the living children before us, and the imperative to do something for them is overwhelming. Using the Government as the instrument is irresistibly encompassing, efficient, and quick. What we cannot see, and refuse even to contemplate in the mind's eye, is the ways in which these same policies, indirectly but just as concretely, create children with needs and with pain. What someday we must acknowledge is that these policies in the end create more pain than they alleviate.

Stop Thinking as Engineers

When it comes to policy, Frank Field is the iconoclast and the optimist, moving far afield from Labour doctrine in order to engineer schemes for dealing with single-parent families and integrating young men back into the labour force. I admire the energy and the imagination that go into those schemes, but I react with the perspective of a person who for 12 years made his living by evaluating such programmes on contract to various departments of the US federal government. There are stacks of such evaluations — of employment programmes, programmes for single parents and every other conceivable kind of programme, some of them as imaginative and energetic as Field's, tried in the States from 1964 to 1980. The evaluations were mostly written by sympathetic observers who tried their best to tease out whatever evidence of success they could find. Nonetheless, they chronicle virtually unrelieved failure. The reason the programmes failed is not because they were inadequately funded nor because the people who ran them were inadequately talented or motivated. Rather, complex social programmes intended to change human behaviour tend not to work out the way they were planned. We are not going to make progress until we stop thinking as engineers, and instead return to think of society as an organism that must be allowed to return to health.

That 'old Burkean rag' yet once again, Professor Deakin says. Actually, Deakin seems drawn himself to local autonomy, but he worries about the ways in which little platoons can become small tyrannies. When he writes 'neighbourhood autonomy by all means, but not through the imposition of artificial homogeneity of values, class composition, or even race', I agree wholeheartedly. I suspect, however, that we have different conceptions of how 'artificial homogeneity' comes about.

Small Tyrannies

But let me address the problem of small tyrannies more directly. My proposition is that humans acting in a private capacity *if restrained from the use of force* have a remarkably good history. To test this, I would ask you to pick your favourite image of people acting oppressively. Now ask: under what conditions were these villains able to do these bad things for a long time without the connivance of the state, without special laws or privileges being granted on their behalf, and without being allowed by the state (if only turning a blind eye) to use physical coercion? I suggest that the longer we consider each specific instance that comes to mind, the more plausible we find this rule of thumb: it is really very difficult for people — including large associations of people and huge corporations — to do anything very bad, for very long, when they are not buttressed by the threat of physical coercion. Private oppression deprived of access to force withers away rather rapidly.

Deakin then wonders how the 'degrading' but essential work is to be done in my autonomous neighbourhoods, wondering if the 'wretches' will have to be imported unless the community resorts to authoritarian methods. He finds it 'dispiriting that an American, of all people, should be preaching the virtues of a static form of society composed of neatly docketed and differentiated small units from which the dangerous classes have been carefully excluded'. Perhaps we have arrived at last to that difference between Americans and the British which I tried to keep in mind as I wrote *Underclass*, for I cannot imagine what kind of communities Professor Deakin has experienced that lead him to those extraordinary assumptions about how communities work.

Autonomous Communities

When I think of autonomous communities, I think of the mid-western town where I grew up. I remember school rooms where the children of corporate executives were best buddies with the children of assembly line workers, church congregations in which every social class was mixed, children growing up thinking that being a garbage collector or a cleaning lady or a janitor was respectable, because the first lesson we were taught was that the only degrading kind of work was no work. I also remember children leaving that community — my wife and I were two of them — into every sort of profession, every corner of the country and the world, in a veritable riot of social and economic mobility. This is 'static'? This is 'neatly docketed'? This is exclusionary and authoritarian? Perhaps I lived in an idyllic community and am thereby misled. But we must consider also the possibility that this is the way that communities of free people tend to function, and that to achieve a society of such communities requires not that governments engineer them, but that governments get out of the way.

CHESTER COLLEGE LIBRARY